University of Alberta

# ROSE GARDENING
## ON THE PRAIRIES

by
George W. Shewchuk

Faculty of Extension
University of Alberta

ISBN:             0-88864-140-0

## THE PRODUCTION TEAM

| | |
|---|---|
| Managing Editor: | Thom Shaw |
| Editorial Assistants: | Lois Hameister<br>Melanie Eastley-Harbourne |
| Graphic Artist: | Melanie Eastley-Harbourne |
| Data Entry: | Arlene Connolly<br>Barbra Jones |
| Macintosh Computer Consultant | Craig Lindsay |
| Technical Reviewer: | Gail Rankin |
| Printing: | U of A Printing Services |

# PREFACE

My interest in roses stretches back 25 years. The first two or three years of trying to grow roses were abysmal failures, in spite of following the advice given in many publications, and the instructions on packaged roses.

My search for a practical method of wintering tender roses was a long one. I visited many private gardens, as well as the research stations at Beaverlodge, Lacombe, Brooks, Morden, and Ottawa. However, the real breakthrough came when I heard the CBC Winnipeg "Prairie Gardener", Stan Westaway, describe what Percy Wright had been doing for some twenty odd years in the development of hardy roses. Robert Simonet of Edmonton had been doing similar work. The research done at Morden has, perhaps, attained the most success to date. In due time, no doubt, we will have some worthy, hardy Hybrid Tea type roses from these sources.

However, there is sufficient proof that even tender roses can be grown successfully in the harshest agricultural areas of Canada. There is no longer any mystery to growing roses on the Prairies. **They are easy to grow, provided they are pampered a little at the correct times.** Inspired by the successful method I found twenty years ago, I have increased the size of my rose beds to include over 350 Hybrid Tea, Grandiflora, Floribunda, Polyantha, and Miniature roses.

It is always a thrill when you discover the first bloom on your new rose bush. It is an even greater thrill when the same bush does well the following year and for several years thereafter. I promise you a beautiful rose garden, provided you follow the advice given in this book. When my suggestions help people grow roses more successfully, I realize my 25 years of work have not been in vain.

From lack of knowledge, many gardeners treat tender roses as annuals, not bothering to protect them over winter, and simply replacing them with new bushes each year. Many other gardeners become discouraged and give up growing roses altogether. This book is written especially for them.

George W. Shewchuk

George W. Shewchuk

# CONTENTS

# CONTENTS *(Continued)*

# CONTENTS *(Continued)*

# FIGURES

# FIGURES *(Continued)*

# FIGURES *(Continued)*

# TABLES

# INTRODUCTION

The rose has been called the "Queen of Flowers". For at least two thousand years, it has enjoyed a universal appeal unequalled by any other flower. Since the beginning of recorded history, roses have been symbolic of romance and love and have been present for all types of special occasions.

Sean McCann, a prominent Irish rose grower in Dublin, says, "The rose is still the best and cheapest plant on the market." Even at twice the price, I certainly agree. Another avid rose grower in the U.S.A., Florence Coates, says, "There's always room for beauty—room for another rose." Roses certainly make the quality of life far better.

## WHY GROW ROSES?

It is no wonder the rose is such a popular flower. For variety of color, fragrance, and continuity of bloom, no other flower compares with the rose. You can count on a generous supply of blooms from early June throughout summer, until the hard frost nips them in October or November. Few other ornamental plants grow under so many different climatic and soil conditions. You don't have to wait years for results because roses bloom the first year they are planted. Many people do not consider their gardens complete without roses.

Roses are available in a variety of sizes: from the tiny 15 cm (6 in.) Miniatures up to some of the tall 2 m (6 ft.) Grandifloras and Hybrid Teas. They can be grown as permanent clumps in a flower bed; they look good against a board fence or a stone wall. Where space is limited, roses can be grown in a border, along a path, under a picture window, or in groups along a foundation. They can be grown in containers on a balcony or patio, and the Miniatures can be grown indoors or out.

You will not have an abundance of roses by just sitting in the shade. To successfully grow roses on the Prairies, you must apply a few fundamentals. At first, they may seem demanding, even overwhelming, but with a bit of practice, these procedures can be accomplished with relative ease. The author's 350 roses receive an average of about three hours of maintenance each week throughout the growing season.

# HOW TO USE ROSES

## ROSES IN THE LANDSCAPE

Roses can be used for landscaping in a number of ways. How they are used is determined by their class, hardiness, height and color, and the ability of certain classes to flower continuously. First determine what you want the roses to do in the landscape, and then select the appropriate variety. A few ways roses can be used and what they will do for the landscape are outlined below.

### ROSE BEDS

One popular way of growing roses is in a totally filled bed. Roses in a bed are more durable, more beautiful, and cheaper substitutes for the once favored annual bedding plants. Floribundas, Grandifloras, and Hybrid Teas make a spectacular show in a single bed, especially when one variety or color is used. This is ideal if you have a large garden area where several beds can be made. If you have a small garden and wish to grow many cultivars, you must sacrifice the masses of color, and get to know many cultivars intimately. One way to partially get around this is to group roses of similar color together, but you must know your rose cultivars well to do this successfully.

Miniature roses mix well with many other annuals in flower beds. For bloom production they are hard to beat. They bloom from early spring until frost.

Massed plantings in beds can create interesting and beautiful pockets in landscape and foundation plantings. They are equally effective when grown in some out-of-the-way garden location to serve as a source of cut flowers.

### HEDGES

Certain rose cultivars are perfect when a natural, free growing type of hedge is required. Roses are not suitable for a tall, narrow hedge or one that is squared off. They may be planted in one or more rows as desired, using one cultivar or a mixture of cultivars. The choice of cultivar or variety for a hedge depends to a large extent on how much time you have. If you wish to have a beautiful, colorful hedge, plant remontant (continuous flowering), Floribunda or Shrub roses (see Table 2, SUMMARY OF ROSE CHARACTERISTICS). However, when Floribundas are chosen, you must use the **winter protection methods** recommended in this book. Interesting groupings can be used in a two row hedge. Illustrations in Figure 1, ROSE HEDGES, give two possible ideas.

### GROUND COVER

In the last few years, many low-growing hardy cultivars have been developed which serve very well as ground covers. Some such roses are so aggressive that no other low-growing plant is able to invade the occupied area. While serving as ground covers, they also produce a profusion of blooms.

Cultivars suitable for ground covers include:
- Bonica
- Charles Albanel
- Ralph's Creeper
- The Fairy

Charles Albanel is considered the hardiest.

### PERENNIAL BORDER

A perennial border can be made of roses alone or in combination with other herbaceous plants. Roses offer a variety of heights and colors to make many interesting possibilities. Grouping of three to five bushes of a variety give spectacular results.

Roses may be used in place of peonies and delphiniums, for example, because certain cultivars supply a longer continuity of bloom. This also applies to other commonly used perennial flowers.

Figure 1
ROSE HEDGES

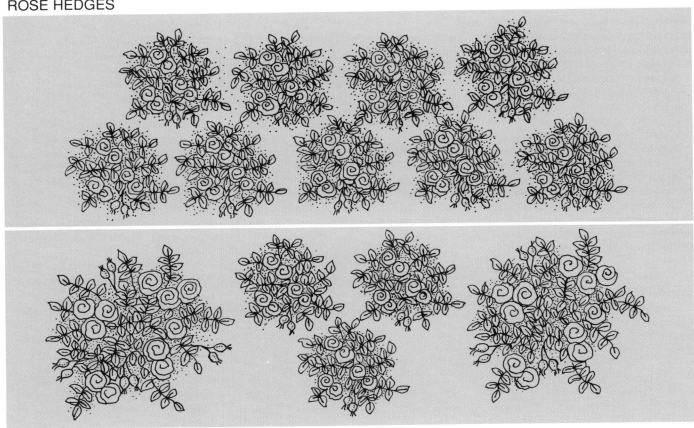

Figure 2
LARGE CONTAINER (RAISED BED)

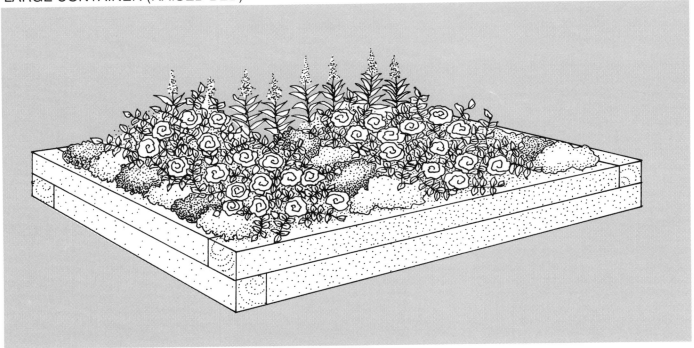

## FOUNDATION PLANTING

Shrub roses, which are much hardier and easier to grow because they require no special winter protection, are commonly used in landscaping and foundation plantings. However, with improved wintering techniques, some very commendable foundation plantings using Hybrid Teas, Grandifloras, and Floribundas can be achieved.

## CONTAINERS

Roses are ideal for planters, boxes, pots, and hanging baskets. However, container size must be carefully matched to the rose's growth or habit to achieve optimum results (see Figure 2, LARGE CONTAINER [RAISED BED]).

Container grown roses can add interesting accent points when placed strategically about the garden or patio. Table 1, ROSES SUITABLE FOR CONTAINER GROWING, lists cultivars adapted to container growth. For those living in town houses and condominiums with only a balcony, it is the only way to grow roses outdoors. See the section GROWING ROSES IN CONTAINERS for details on the growth needs of roses in containers.

# OTHER USES

## ARRANGEMENTS

Remember the elegance associated with a party, banquet, etc. when there is a large arrangement of roses on a table. Very few flowers enhance the occasion more than an arrangement of roses.

## BOUQUET

A bouquet is simply a number of long-stemmed roses, in no special arrangement, with their stems tied together. A dozen roses of a single color make a very generous and impressive bouquet.

No one will deny that there are few things as heart-warming as receiving a bouquet of roses from a loved one.

## DRIED ROSE BLOOMS

Drying rose blooms is quite a popular hobby. If you are interested, obtain a good manual from a hobby shop on how to preserve flowers. Rose shows often have beautiful exhibits of dried miniature roses. This is the perfect place to gain information on the processes and arrangements.

## PERFUME CRAFTING

Cologne, rose water, and fragrant oil can be made from rose petals. Tom Thumb workshops, Box 3496 A.R. Alexandria, VA 22302, U.S.A., has a recipe for making them.

## BOUTONNIERE or CORSAGE

Have you ever noticed how proudly a rose corsage is worn? Need more be said? Contrary to common practice, a corsage is to be worn with flowers pointing upward, and if there is a ribbon or bow, it should be at the bottom of the corsage.

## SINGLE CUT FLOWER

A single rose in a suitable container (a crystal vase) epitomizes true, simple natural beauty. A single, simple rose makes a clear statement of admiration. Its unique sweet fragrance and simple beauty is unsurpassed by any other flower.

**Thank You, Happy Birthday, Happy Anniversary, I Love You, Retirement, Congratulations** can all be said eloquently with roses. If you are looking for a unique way to say

## Table 1
# ROSES SUITABLE FOR CONTAINER GROWING

| HYBRID TEA | FLORIBUNDAS | MINIATURES "hanging basket" | MINIATURES | POLYANTHAS |
|---|---|---|---|---|
| Granada (scarlet, yellow) | Gene Boerner (pink) | Baby Darling (apricot blend) | Red Cascade (dark red) | Cecile Brunner (very light pink) |
| Double Delight (red, creamy white) | Bon Bon (pink blend) | Starina (orange red) | Pink Cameo (medium pink) | The Fairy (light pink) |
| Oregold (yellow) | Coventry Cathedral (apricot blend) | Beauty Scarlet (medium red) | | Dopey (medium red) |
| Seashell (apricot blend) | Eutin (dark red) | Gold Coin (dark yellow) | | China Doll (medium pink) |
| | Golden Slippers (yellow blend) | Mr. Bluebird (dark lavender) | | |
| | Morden Cardinette (cardinal red) | | | |

something appropriate on any special occasion, say it with roses. What nicer way is there to be remembered than with roses!

## ROSE WINE

Rose hips or petals make a delectable and a highly prized wine. Most wine recipe books give adequate instructions on making these wines.

## ROSE PETAL TEA

Tea made from fragrant rose petals is a delicacy. A small handful of fresh fragrant rose petals in an average tea pot (4 - 5 cups) makes a unique and delicious tea. The best petals are from the native Alberta Rose growing in a remote area free of possible chemical residue from field crop and roadside spraying for weeds, insects, and

diseases. Native wild rose petals have a strong pleasant fragrance. Rose petals may be dried and kept for future use in an air-tight container.

CAUTION: Roses are often sprayed or dusted with toxic chemicals to protect them from disease and insect damage. No one should risk ingesting potentially hazardous chemicals. If roses can be grown without the use of insecticides and fungicides, go ahead and make the wine or tea.

## ROSES AS HOUSE PLANTS

Roses make interesting and beautiful plants when grown in a bright, sunny window, or under artificial lights.

When you grow roses in the home, humidity problems are usually encountered during the winter months.

To help relieve this problem, the "Gravel Tray" technique may be used. A shallow tray is filled with marble-sized pebbles about 3 cm (1.25 in.) deep. Pour water into the tray until it rises to within 1 cm (0.50 in.) of the top of the pebbles. Place the potted roses on top of the pebbles. As the water in the bottom of the tray evaporates, it provides some of the humidity necessary for the plants.

The most suitable roses for house plants are those commonly used as Mother's Day gifts. Many types of potted roses are commonly seen on the market around Mother's Day.

Further information on this subject may be found under the section, GROWING UNDER ARTIFICIAL LIGHTS.

# GROWING ROSES

Roses are perennial plants and thus expected to last for several years. Before you even start digging, there are many things to consider. This section of the book is a simple guide for avoiding serious pitfalls.

## SELECTING ROSES

If you are inexperienced, selecting roses can be a bewildering experience when you browse through a busy market place or study a rose catalogue. This chapter is written to assist you to find and buy the best.

### TYPES OF BUSH ROSES

Roses are available in at least 45 different classes. The most common rose classes grown on the Prairies include:
- Hybrid Tea
- Floribunda
- Grandiflora
- Polyantha
- Climbing
- Ramblers
- Miniature
- Moss
- Shrub
- Sweetheart
- Standard Tree

NOTE: The Standard Tree rose is a specimen with multiple grafts on a tall rose cane.

### HYBRID TEA ROSES

The most popular of all the roses are Hybrid Tea roses. These plants grow into small bushes from 45 - 90 cm (18 - 36 in.). The popular Hybrid Teas have long pointed buds and high centered blooms with strong, straight stems. They make excellent show roses and are usually the type sold by florists. Most are double-blossomed; they bear anywhere from 20 - 70 velvet textured petals. A few Hybrid Tea cultivars such as Dainty Bess, White Wings, Safrano, and Command Performance have single and semi-double blossoms and from 5 - 20 petals.

The leaves of Hybrid Tea roses are generally dark or medium green. A few cultivars start their new foliage as dark red, then turn to green. Their texture varies from glossy and leathery to dull in appearance.

Hybrid Tea roses can now be obtained in almost any color or color combination. They are suitable for planting in a bed or in groups in a border to supplement other plantings.

### FLORIBUNDA ROSES

Floribundas first originated from crosses made with Polyanthas and Hybrid Teas in 1922. The flowers of Floribunda bushes come in clusters of single or double bloom on each stem. They are everblooming and present a wonderful display starting in June and ending with the arrival of killing frost in the fall.

Floribundas are similar in height to Hybrid Teas, but are considered slightly hardier. Each year, more and better Floribundas are developed. Because of their profusion and consistency of bloom, they have become increasingly more popular since the 1940's. They are excellent for use where an abundance of color is desired.

### GRANDIFLORA ROSES

Grandifloras are hybrids resulting from crosses made between Floribundas and Hybrid Tea roses in 1955. This crossing combined the good qualities of the free flowering Floribundas with the magnificent long stemmed Hybrid Teas. The flowers come in clusters that are only slightly smaller than the Hybrid Teas. The stems are longer than those of the Floribundas. The buds and flowers resemble those of Hybrid Tea roses and are suitable for cutting. If disbudded early, you would need an expert to tell the difference between the two.

### POLYANTHA ROSES

Polyanthas came into prominence in the 1930's and 1940's when florists began growing them in pots as gifts for Easter and Mother's Day. The most popular cultivars are Cecile Brunner, Cameo, Margo Koster, Mothersday, Dopey, The Fairy, China Doll, Happy, and Sparkler. They produce a greater profusion of bloom and far longer bloom period than any other rose. They come in various bush sizes ranging in height from 40 - 90 cm (16 - 36 in.). Another distinct type in this class is the Dwarf Polyantha growing from 30 - 45 cm (12 - 18 in.). These produce flowers in compact clusters from stems of different stages of maturity which ensures a steady supply of flowers. The blooms are small and do not exceed 5 cm (2 in.) in diameter.

### CLIMBING AND RAMBLER ROSES

In mild climates, Climbing and Rambler roses are grown to cover walls and arches, or because of their long climbing branches, to form backgrounds and screens.

Some of the best climbing roses on the Prairies are grown by Mr. Wilhelm Kronschage of Stony Plain, Alberta. His two roses are trained on an archway. In late fall, the canes are carefully taken off the archway and curled on the ground around the base. Then the canes are weighted down with bricks or rocks and covered with a bit of soil. On top of this, 60 cm (2 ft.) of potato tops, lawn clippings, leaves, and other garden material that can be picked up in the process of a fall garden clean-up are added. Considerable care is taken to avoid breaking the canes because climbing roses generally bloom on last year's growth.

The cultivars Blaze, Danse du Feu (Spectacular), Morning Jewel, and Rosarium Uetersen appear to be the hardiest of the climbers. Patricia Macoun is the hardiest of the ramblers.

### MINIATURE ROSES

Miniature roses are everblooming replicas of Hybrid Teas that can be as small as the tip of your small finger to about 3 - 4 cm (1.5 in.) across. Plant sizes vary from 15 - 45 cm (6 - 18 in.) in height. Most have little or no fragrance. Despite their size, they are as easy to winter as the Hybrid Teas. They are also popular as potted plants and can be grown indoors or outdoors.

## MOSS ROSES

Moss roses get their name from the tiny hair-like glands that cover the sepals and sometimes the terminal parts of stems that resemble moss. This growth is sticky and gives off a resinous aroma like that of balsam fir. They range in size from 1 - 2 m (3 - 6 ft.) down to the 15 cm (6 in.) miniatures.

## SHRUB ROSES

Shrub roses are able to survive our winters without any special protection and therefore are characterized by their hardiness. This class is used rather loosely. Rosarians use it as a "catch-all" for cultivars that do not fit in any of the commonly recognized classes. Shrub roses vary in size (depending on the

## Figure 3
## STANDARD TREE ROSE

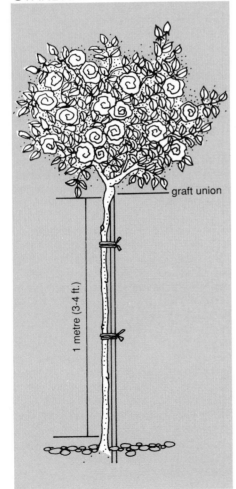

graft union

1 metre (3-4 ft.)

cultivar) from 60 - 180 cm (2 - 6 ft.). Many of the older cultivars bloom only once during the spring. Newly developed cultivars bloom almost continuously from spring until fall. They include the Rugosa cultivars, plus the Hybrid Foetida, Hybrid Spinosissima, and the many other hybrids related to the Japanese and Altai rose.

Shrub roses are commonly used in combination with other shrubs in landscaping. They can be given the same general care as the other shrubs and do not require any special planting method.

## SWEETHEART ROSES

In this type of rose, the individual florets show the perfection of form of the Hybrid Tea rose but are very much smaller. A typical cultivar in this category is the Polyantha, Cecile Brunner. There are currently many miniature roses that also may fall into this category.

## STANDARD TREE ROSES

Standard Tree roses are usually Hybrid Tea roses that have been grafted onto a tall briar stock about 1 m (3 ft.) from the ground (see Figure 3, STANDARD TREE ROSE). This gives the appearance of a small tree. This can also be done with Grandifloras and Floribundas.

A similar thing can also be done with miniatures, where the roses are grafted onto a shorter stock 30 - 60 cm (1 - 2 ft.) in height.

## GUIDE TO BUYING ROSES

You can never know how well a rose will do simply by looking at the pictures on the package or in the catalogue. There is general agreement that the best way to choose your roses is to see them growing in your neighborhood or in local nurseries. Attending rose shows can be very helpful in selecting rose types, colors, or cultivars you like.

A very useful guide to assist in rose selection is Table 2, SUMMARY OF ROSE CHARACTERISTICS. Review the LEGEND at the end of the table for a

description of the abbreviations used within the table.

The first requirement for successful rose growing is to purchase plants of good quality. You can be quite confident of getting strong, healthy, well-rooted plants if you buy them by mail order from any of the major, reputable rose nurseries (see MAIL ORDER SUPPLIERS in the RESOURCE MATERIALS section). These nurseries pack the dormant bushes in a water-proof wrapping, which keeps them from drying out. Generally you will receive them in top shape (see Figure 4, PACKAGED ROSES; unpruned vs. pruned roots).

Over the past few years, you may have noticed that you have been unable to buy roses with a good sized root system from some department stores and garden centers. What you get are rose bushes with severely pruned roots (see Figure 5, ROSE WITH PRUNED ROOTS). Given a choice between the amputated roots in a small box with a handful of wood shavings and one with all its roots intact from a nursery, take the latter. No reliable nursery would deliberately cut 75

## Figure 4
## PACKAGED ROSES (unpruned vs. pruned roots)

Figure 5
ROSE WITH PRUNED ROOTS

Figure 6
ROSE WITH UNPRUNED
ROOTS

percent of the roots off its trees and shrubs. They know that good roots are essential for getting the plant off to a good start. In the short season and harsh climate on the Prairies, roses must have as much of their roots intact as possible. From personal experience and scientific research, rose growers know that plants with a good root system take much less time to get established and bloom, than those with a severely cropped root system (see Figure 6, ROSE WITH UNPRUNED ROOTS). The American Rose Magazine recently listed several rose societies that complained about this problem and threatened to boycott firms that practice heavy root pruning.

Each spring, many firms get on the gardening bandwagon by selling roses, other selected ornamentals, and bedding plants. Also, thousands of plants are ruined by inexperienced, careless, and uninformed management and sales people. Often rose bushes are put on exhibit outdoors for sale in early April and in a few days are dead from repeated freezing and thawing. To the amazement of knowledgeable gardeners, these dead roses are held on display and sold to unwary customers long after their demise. The author once drew a sales lady's attention to dead roses being sold. In defence she stated, "Oh, we have a 90-day warranty on them. If they don't grow within that period, return them with the purchase slip and we will return your money." Is it any wonder that people tell you they just cannot grow roses, or that they are reluctant to try growing them again?

Many people who scorn buying day-old bread or wilted lettuce, will deliberately postpone buying roses until $1.49 day. By this time many of the plants will have suffered and dried out beyond any hope of a healthy recovery. Many may also have begun to leaf out or produce long, slender, green sprouts. A plant in this condition is not a prime specimen. **You cannot grow quality blooms from inferior stock.**

Knowledgeable managers of retail outlets know that packaged roses are perishable, and develop well-planned facilities to provide proper care and display areas. In addition, informed personnel are employed to properly care for the plants until they are sold. These are the only outlets that the shrewd rose gardener should patronize.

If you are going to buy packaged roses, purchase them as soon as they arrive at the dealers. If it's too early for planting, store them in a cool place like a root cellar, produce room, or garage kept just a few degrees above freezing. The roses can be stored unharmed for a week or two. They can also be heeled-in as described under the HEELING IN section.

A healthy rose plant has a green, plump look about it. Do not confuse the green wax protective coating with the appearance of a healthy plant. The plant should have a least three hefty stems of reasonable length. The buds should be plainly visible. The bark on the canes should not be wrinkled or withered. There should be no sprouts longer than 12 mm (0.5 in.) or any indication of sprouts having been removed.

### ROSE GRADES

Another guide for buying roses often overlooked or not known to many is **grade**. Rose bushes are graded just like eggs, butter, or potatoes. A No. 1 rose carries three or more stout 45 cm (18 in.) canes; No. 1.5, two 38 cm (15 in.) canes; No. 2, two 30 cm (12 in.) canes. Quite common on the market are ungraded roses marked, "two year old, field grown". If you have a choice, No. 1 grade is generally the best buy (see Figure 7, HYBRID TEA ROSE GRADES).

### IMPORTANCE OF WAXING

If there is a choice between roses with waxed canes or unwaxed canes, choose the waxed specimens. Waxing helps to prevent the rapid dehydration that can occur from the time they are packaged to the time they are planted. Tests conducted in the U.S.A. have proven that bushes with waxed canes consistently out perform the unwaxed specimens. They establish themselves much faster and produce more blossoms. This effect is evident even in the second year of growth.

### SPROUTED ROSES

Avoid buying heavily sprouted roses.

## Figure 7
## HYBRID TEA ROSE GRADES

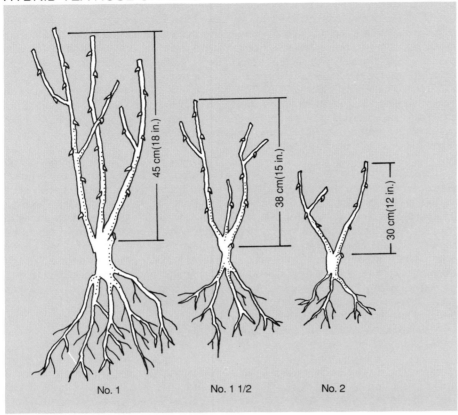

No. 1      45 cm (18 in.)

No. 1 1/2      38 cm (15 in.)

No. 2      30 cm (12 in.)

Retailers often receive their rose shipment with sprouts of up to 15 cm (6 in.) on their plants. It then requires a crew of employees to hastily take them off to ready them for sale. It takes a rose gardener with a bit of experience to detect bushes that have had their sprouts removed.

Avoid planting rose bushes with sprouts longer than 5 cm (2 in.). If you have no choice, remove the sprouts prior to planting them. This is not necessarily the best thing for the rose bush, but it is the lesser of two evils. You can remove the sprouts and allow the bush to expend its remaining energy on the new shoots, or leave the sprouts on and have the bush expend much of its energy on sprouts it may eventually lose anyway.

The tender sprouts need as much protection as possible from frost, wind, heat, or sun-scald. The sprouts need to be hardened off so they can withstand these natural elements without injury. This can be easily done by covering

them with a burlap sack. This porous cover is retained for a week to 10 days during which time the sprouts green up. Remove the cover for short periods on cloudy, calm, or rainy days to permit gradual adjustment. When fully greened up, the cover can be permanently removed.

Some people prefer to protect and harden off their rose bushes by mounding the bushes with soil when they are planted. When the sprouts begin to appear through the mound, the soil can be gradually removed to get the shoots hardened off fully .

### POTTED ROSES

A safer way for the novice to buy roses is to choose specimens that are already potted. You can tell at a glance whether or not the bush is growing and healthy in appearance. Another advantage is that they may be planted in late spring or summer, when planting of dormant bushes is neither feasible, nor practical.

On the other hand, they cost more and offer no other particular advantage if planting can be done in early spring.

### GOOD CULTIVARS TO START WITH

Each year new roses are being added to the already comprehensive list of nearly 16,000 cultivars, and older mediocre cultivars are being down graded. Keep in mind that rose performance rating changes with time. However, some like Peace, Chrysler Imperial, and Queen Elizabeth have been around for more than 25 years and are still looked upon as the top roses. Over the last few years, however, many newly introduced roses are giving them a good run for their money.  Also in the field of new roses is the development of cultivars resistant to mildew, blackspot, and severe winter conditions. Canadian hybridist, Henry Marshall, at Morden, Manitoba has developed two hardy Floribunda-type roses. The Adelaide Hoodless and Cuthbert Grant are already available through some Prairie nurseries. Also developed over the last few years are Amorette, Cardinette, and Morden Centennial. These cultivars came through our severe winters without the special planting and wintering instructions outlined here for tender roses.

What roses should you plant? This is a personal thing. Some like to show; others like cut roses for the house; while others wish to have roses in the landscape. Do your own thing with the full spectrum of roses. In Table 2, SUMMARY OF ROSE CHARACTERISTICS, you will find a listing of good roses that you can rely on for performance and beauty.

The column labelled "George's Choice" includes proven roses that have done well over a period of years for many people throughout the country.

### SOME SOURCES OF GOOD ROSES

In the author's experience, the best place to purchase roses is from a reputable mail order supply house. It is best to order early when the supply is plentiful so that you do not have to accept substitutes. The best time to order your roses is before the end of the year and not later than January. You should also request that they be shipped to arrive between April 24 - 30.

Some of the quality mail order suppliers are listed in the RESOURCE MATERIALS section. If you are considering importing roses the procedure is also outlined in the RESOURCE MATERIALS section.

If you intend purchasing roses at a local gardening supply outlet, make certain that you get them as soon as the shipment arrives. If necessary, you can possibly hold your roses for a week or two by following the instructions given under the HEELING IN section. Do not buy roses with dried canes or long sprouts even if they are reduced to clear.

## THE BEST ROSES

What are the best roses? This is a very difficult question to answer. Perhaps the best way to answer this is to have you consult Table 2, SUMMARY OF ROSE CHARACTERISTICS. In order to understand the symbols used in this table, the LEGEND at the end of the table should be consulted. In particular, review the cultivars listed under "George's Choice" and "The Top Fifty" columns.

Table 2
## SUMMARY OF ROSE CHARACTERISTICS

| ROSE CLASSES and CULTIVARS | ARS RATING | HEIGHT | COLOR | BLOSSOM SIZE | BLOSSOM TYPE | BLOSSOM FORM | CONTINUITY OF BLOOM | FRAGRANCE | PERFORMANCE AT ROSE SHOWS | HARDINESS for the PRAIRIES | GEORGE'S CHOICE | THE TOP FIFTY |
|---|---|---|---|---|---|---|---|---|---|---|---|---|
| **HYBRID TEA (HT)** | | | | | | | | | | | | |
| Adolf Horstman | 6.2 | m | yb | L | 3 | p | bbb | f | B | 2 | • | |
| Alaska Centennial | 7.2 | m | mr | L | 3 | p | bbb | f | B | 2 | • | |
| Alec's Red | 7.8 | m | mr | L | 3 | p | bb | f | A | 2 | | |
| Alpine Sunset | 7.4 | s | ab | L | 3 | cu | bbb | fff | B | 2 | | |
| Amazing Grace | N | m | mp | L | 3 | p | bb | f | B | 2 | | |
| American Heritage | 7.0 | m | yb | L | 3 | p | bb | - | B | 2 | | |
| Apricot Nectar | 8.1 | m | ab | L | 3 | p | bb | fff | B | 2 | | |
| Apricot Silk | 5.7 | m | ab | L | 3 | p | b | f | B | 2 | | |
| Austragold | N | t | my | L | 3 | p | bbb | f | B | 2 | • | • |
| Ave Maria | N | m | ob | L | 3 | p | bbb | - | B | 2 | • | • |
| Bel Ange | 7.6 | t | mp | M | 3 | p | bbb | fff | B | 2 | • | • |
| Bewitched | 7.2 | m | mp | L | 3 | p | bb | f | B | 2 | • | |
| Big Ben | 7.2 | m | dr | L | 3 | p | bb | fff | A | 2 | | |
| Blue Girl (Kolner Karneval) | 6.4 | m | m | L | 3 | p | bb | - | A | 2 | | |
| Blue Moon | 7.1 | m | m | L | 3 | p | b | - | B | 2 | | |
| Blue Nile | 7.1 | m | m | L | 3 | p | b | - | B | 2 | | |
| Bonnie Scotland | N | m | dp | L | 3 | p | bb | f | B | 2 | | |
| Bonsoir | N | m | mp | L | 3 | p | bb | ff | B | 2 | | |
| Brandy | 7.3 | m | ab | L | 3 | p | bb | - | B | 2 | | |
| Broadway | N | m | yb | L | 3 | p | bb | - | B | 2 | | |
| Burgund '81 (Loving Memory) | 7.5 | m | mr | L | 3 | p | bbb | f | B | 2 | • | • |
| Burnaby | 6.5 | m | w | L | 3 | p | bb | f | B | 2 | | |
| Canadian White Star | N | m | w | L | 3 | p | b | - | A | 2 | | |
| Candy Stripe | 6.6 | m | pb | L | 3 | p | bb | fff | B | 2 | | |
| Capistrano | N | m | mp | L | 3 | p | bb | f | B | 2 | | |
| Charlotte Armstrong | 7.4 | m | dp | L | 3 | p | bb | f | A | 2 | • | • |
| Chicago Peace | 8.4 | t | pb | L | 3 | p | bbb | f | B | 2 | • | • |
| Christian Dior | 7.1 | m | mr | L | 3 | p | bb | - | A | 2 | • | • |
| Chrysler Imperial | 8.2 | m | dr | L | 3 | p | bb | fff | A | 2 | • | • |
| Clivia | N | m | ob | L | 3 | p | bb | f | B | 2 | | |
| Color Magic | 8.0 | m | pb | L | 3 | p | bb | f | A | 2 | • | |
| Command Performance | 7.0 | t | or | L | 3 | p | b | fff | A | 2 | • | |
| Corso | N | m | ob | L | 3 | p | bb | f | B | 2 | • | |
| Crimson Glory | 7.3 | m | dr | L | 3 | p | bb | fff | A | 2 | • | |
| Dainty Bess | 8.6 | m | lp | L | 1 | cu | bb | f | A | 2 | • | |

Table 2
## SUMMARY OF ROSE CHARACTERISTICS *(Continued)*

| ROSE CLASSES and CULTIVARS | ARS RATING | HEIGHT | COLOR | BLOSSOM SIZE | BLOSSOM TYPE | BLOSSOM FORM | CONTINUITY OF BLOOM | FRAGRANCE | PERFORMANCE AT ROSE SHOWS | HARDINESS for the PRAIRIES | GEORGE'S CHOICE | THE TOP FIFTY |
|---|---|---|---|---|---|---|---|---|---|---|---|---|
| Diamond Jubilee | 6.9 | m | yb | L | 3 | cu | bb | f | B | 2 | | |
| Dolly Parton | 7.4 | m | or | L | 3 | p | bb | f | A | 2 | | |
| Doris Tysterman | 7.0 | m | ob | L | 3 | p | bbb | f | B | 2 | • | |
| Double Delight | 9.0 | m | rb | L | 3 | p | bbb | fff | A | 2 | • | • |
| Dr. A.J. Verhage | N | m | dy | L | 3 | p | bb | fff | A | 2 | | |
| Dr. Brownell | 6.5 | m | yb | L | 3 | p | bbb | fff | B | 3 | | |
| Drambuie | N | m | rb | L | 3 | p | bb | ff | B | 2 | | |
| Duet | 8.0 | m | mp | L | 3 | p | bbb | f | A | 2 | • | • |
| Duke of Windsor | 6.7 | m | ob | L | 3 | p | bb | fff | B | 2 | | |
| Dutch Gold | 6.8 | m | my | L | 3 | p | bb | f | B | 2 | | |
| Electron | 8.0 | m | dp | L | 3 | p | bbb | ff | B | 2 | • | • |
| Ena Harkness | 6.3 | m | mr | L | 3 | p | bb | fff | B | 2 | | |
| Ernest E. Morse | 7.2 | m | mr | L | 3 | p | bb | fff | A | 2 | | |
| First Prize | 9.1 | m | pb | L | 3 | p | b | ff | A | 1 | | |
| Florentina | 7.7 | m | dr | L | 3 | p | bb | f | B | 2 | | |
| Folklore | 8.3 | m | ob | L | 3 | p | bb | fff | A | 2 | • | |
| Fragrant Cloud | 8.1 | m | or | L | 3 | p | bb | fff | B | 2 | | |
| Fran Karl Druschki (HP) | 7.6 | m | w | L | 3 | p | bb | - | A | 2 | | |
| Friendship | 7.2 | m | dp | L | 3 | p | b | fff | A | 2 | | |
| Garden Party | 8.8 | m | w | L | 3 | p | bbb | f | A | 2 | • | • |
| Golden Jubilee | N | m | yb | L | 3 | p | bb | f | B | 2 | • | • |
| Gold Medal | N | m | dy | L | 3 | p | bb | - | B | 2 | | |
| Granada | 8.6 | m | rb | L | 3 | cu | bb | fff | A | 2 | • | |
| Grand Masterpiece | 7.0 | m | mr | L | 3 | p | bb | f | B | 2 | | |
| Grandpa Dickson (Irish Gold) | 7.1 | m | my | L | 3 | p | bb | f | A | 2 | | |
| Gypsy | 6.1 | m | or | L | 3 | p | bb | f | B | 2 | | |
| Hawaii | 5.9 | m | or | L | 3 | p | bbb | fff | B | 2 | • | |
| Headliner | N | m | pb | L | 3 | p | bb | f | A | 2 | | |
| Heirloom | 6.8 | m | m | L | 3 | p | b | fff | B | 2 | | |
| Helen Traubel | 6.9 | t | pb | L | 3 | p | bb | f | B | 2 | • | |
| Honor | 7.6 | m | w | L | 3 | p | bbb | ff | B | 2 | • | |
| Ingrid Bergman | 7.3 | m | dr | L | 3 | p | bbb | ff | A | 2 | • | |
| Isabel de Ortiz | 6.6 | m | pb | L | 3 | p | bb | f | B | 2 | | |
| Jadis | 7.3 | m | mp | L | 3 | p | bb | fff | B | 2 | • | |
| John F. Kennedy | 6.2 | m | w | L | 3 | p | bbb | f | B | 2 | | |

Table 2
SUMMARY OF ROSE CHARACTERISTICS *(Continued)*

| ROSE CLASSES and CULTIVARS | ARS RATING | HEIGHT | COLOR | BLOSSOM SIZE | BLOSSOM TYPE | BLOSSOM FORM | CONTINUITY OF BLOOM | FRAGRANCE | PERFORMANCE AT ROSE SHOWS | HARDINESS for the PRAIRIES | GEORGE'S CHOICE | THE TOP FIFTY |
|---|---|---|---|---|---|---|---|---|---|---|---|---|
| John Paul II | N | m | ab | L | 3 | p | b | f | B | 1 | | |
| John Waterer | 7.6 | m | dr | L | 3 | p | bbb | f | B | 2 | • | |
| Josephine Bruce | 6.9 | m | dr | L | 3 | p | bb | fff | B | 2 | | |
| Julia's Rose | 7.4 | m | r | L | 3 | p | bb | f | B | 2 | • | |
| Just Joey | 7.9 | m | ob | L | 3 | p | bb | fff | B | 2 | | |
| Kaiserin Auguste Viktoria | 5.8 | m | w | L | 3 | p | b | fff | B | 2 | | |
| Karl Herbst | 6.6 | m | mr | L | 3 | p | bb | fff | B | 2 | | |
| Keepsake | 7.8 | m | pb | L | 3 | p | bb | - | A | 2 | | |
| King's Ransom | 6.7 | m | dy | L | 3 | p | bb | f | B | 2 | | |
| Korde's Perfecta | 6.9 | m | pb | L | 3 | p | bb | fff | A | 2 | | |
| Lady X | 8.4 | t | pb | L | 3 | p | bb | f | A | 2 | • | |
| Las Vegas | 7.6 | m | ob | L | 3 | p | bb | f | B | 2 | | |
| Lolita | 6.6 | m | ab | L | 3 | p | bbb | fff | B | 2 | • | • |
| Lowell Thomas | 5.0 | m | dy | L | 3 | p | bbb | f | B | 2 | | |
| Madras | 7.5 | m | pb | L | 3 | p | bb | f | B | 2 | | |
| Maria Stern | 8.0 | t | ob | L | 3 | p | bb | ff | B | 2 | • | |
| Matador | 7.9 | m | ob | L | 3 | p | bb | - | B | 2 | | |
| May Lyon | N | m | dp | L | 3 | p | bbb | f | B | 2 | • | |
| Michelle Meilland | 7.6 | m | lp | L | 3 | p | bb | - | B | 2 | • | |
| Milestone | 7.8 | m | rb | L | 3 | p | bbb | - | A | 2 | • | |
| Mirandy | 6.1 | m | dr | L | 3 | p | bb | fff | A | 2 | | |
| Mischief | 7.4 | m | ob | L | 3 | p | bb | ff | B | 2 | | |
| Miss All American Beauty | 8.5 | m | dp | L | 3 | p | bbb | ff | A | 2 | • | • |
| Mister Lincoln | 9.1 | t | dr | L | 3 | p | bb | fff | A | 2 | • | • |
| Miss Canada | 5.4 | m | pb | L | 3 | p | bb | f | B | 2 | • | |
| Mojave | 6.2 | m | ob | L | 3 | p | bb | f | A | 2 | | |
| Mon Cheri | 7.8 | m | rb | L | 3 | p | b | f | A | 1 | | |
| National Trust | 7.3 | m | dr | L | 3 | p | b | - | B | 2 | | |
| New Day | 6.6 | m | my | L | 3 | p | bb | fff | B | 2 | | |
| Norita | 6.5 | m | dr | L | 3 | p | b | f | B | 2 | | |
| Oklahoma | 6.2 | m | dr | L | 3 | p | bb | fff | B | 2 | • | |
| Olympiad | 8.1 | m | mr | L | 3 | p | b | fff | A | 2 | | |
| Olympic Torch | 6.9 | m | rb | L | 3 | p | bb | ff | B | 2 | | |
| Oregold | 7.4 | m | dy | L | 3 | p | bb | f | B | 2 | | |
| Oriana | 7.0 | m | rb | L | 3 | p | bbb | ff | A | 2 | • | • |

Table 2
SUMMARY OF ROSE CHARACTERISTICS *(Continued)*

| ROSE CLASSES and CULTIVARS | ARS RATING | HEIGHT | COLOR | BLOSSOM SIZE | BLOSSOM TYPE | BLOSSOM FORM | CONTINUITY OF BLOOM | FRAGRANCE | PERFORMANCE AT ROSE SHOWS | HARDINESS for the PRAIRIES | GEORGE'S CHOICE | THE TOP FIFTY |
|---|---|---|---|---|---|---|---|---|---|---|---|---|
| Osiria | 7.4 | m | rb | L | 3 | p | bb | fff | A | 2 | • | |
| Papa Meilland | 7.4 | m | dr | L | 3 | p | bb | fff | A | 2 | • | |
| Paradise | 8.8 | m | mr | L | 3 | p | b | f | A | 2 | | |
| Pascali | 8.7 | m | w | L | 3 | p | bb | f | A | 2 | • | • |
| Peace | 8.9 | m | yb | L | 3 | p | bbb | ff | A | 2 | • | • |
| Peer Gynt | 6.3 | m | yb | L | 3 | p | bbb | f | B | 2 | • | |
| Perfume Delight | 7.8 | m | mp | L | 3 | p | bb | fff | B | 2 | | |
| Peter Frankenfeld | 7.8 | m | dp | L | 3 | p | bbb | f | A | 2 | • | • |
| Pink Peace | 7.5 | m | mp | L | 3 | p | bb | fff | B | 2 | • | |
| Piroschka | N | m | mp | L | 3 | p | bb | f | B | 2 | | |
| Portrait | 7.2 | m | pb | L | 3 | p | bbb | f | B | 2 | • | • |
| Precious Platinum | 8.1 | m | mr | L | 3 | p | bb | f | A | 2 | • | |
| Prima Ballerina | 6.9 | m | dp | L | 3 | p | b | fff | B | 2 | | |
| Princess Margaret of England | 7.4 | m | mp | L | 3 | p | bb | ff | B | 2 | | |
| Pristine* | 8.9 | m | w | L | 3 | p | bbb | f | A | 2 | | |
| Proud Land | 7.1 | m | dr | L | 3 | p | b | f | B | 2 | | |
| Queen O' the Lakes | 7.7 | m | dr | L | 3 | cu | bbb | ff | C | 3 | • | • |
| Red Devil | 7.6 | m | mr | L | 3 | p | b | f | A | 2 | | |
| Red Jacket | 8.0 | m | mr | L | 3 | p | b | f | B | 2 | | |
| Red Lion | 7.3 | m | mr | L | 3 | p | b | - | A | 2 | | |
| Red Queen | 7.0 | m | mr | L | 3 | p | bbb | f | B | 2 | • | • |
| Red Masterpiece | 6.7 | m | dr | L | 3 | p | bb | fff | B | 2 | | |
| Remember Me | N | m | ob | L | 3 | p | bb | f | B | 2 | | |
| Rose Gaujard | 5.9 | m | rb | L | 3 | p | bb | fff | A | 2 | • | |
| Royal Alberta Hall | N | m | rb | L | 3 | p | bb | fff | A | 2 | | |
| Royal Canadian | 5.7 | m | mr | L | 3 | p | bb | ff | B | 2 | | |
| Royal Dane (Troika) | 6.8 | t | ob | L | 3 | p | bbb | fff | B | 2 | • | • |
| Royal Highness | 8.6 | m | lp | L | 3 | p | b | ff | A | 1 | • | |
| Seashell | 7.4 | m | ob | L | 3 | ca | bb | f | A | 2 | • | |
| Sheer Bliss | N | m | w | L | 3 | p | bbb | f | A | 2 | • | |
| Silver Jubilee | 7.4 | m | pb | L | 3 | p | bb | f | A | 2 | • | |
| Silver Star | 6.3 | m | m | L | 3 | cu | bbb | fff | B | 2 | • | • |
| Smoky | 5.3 | m | rb | L | 3 | p | bb | - | B | 2 | • | |
| Spellbinder | 6.6 | m | pb | L | 3 | p | bb | f | A | 2 | • | |
| Summer Sunshine | 7.0 | m | dy | L | 3 | p | bbb | f | A | 2 | • | |

*bloom very short-lived

## Table 2
## SUMMARY OF ROSE CHARACTERISTICS *(Continued)*

| ROSE CLASSES and CULTIVARS | ARS RATING | HEIGHT | COLOR | BLOSSOM SIZE | BLOSSOM TYPE | BLOSSOM FORM | CONTINUITY OF BLOOM | FRAGRANCE | PERFORMANCE AT ROSE SHOWS | HARDINESS for the PRAIRIES | GEORGE'S CHOICE | THE TOP FIFTY |
|---|---|---|---|---|---|---|---|---|---|---|---|---|
| Sunblest | 7.0 | m | dy | L | 3 | p | bb | f | B | 2 | | |
| Super Star Supreme | 7.0 | m | or | L | 3 | p | bb | ff | B | 2 | | |
| Susan Massu | 7.0 | m | yb | L | 3 | p | bb | - | B | 2 | | |
| Sutter's Gold | 6.5 | m | ob | L | 3 | p | bb | fff | B | 2 | | |
| Swarthmore | 8.5 | m | pb | L | 3 | p | bb | f | A | 2 | • | |
| Tiffany | 8.3 | t | pb | L | 3 | p | bb | fff | A | 2 | • | |
| Toro | 7.9 | m | dr | L | 3 | p | bb | fff | B | 2 | • | |
| Touch of Class | N | m | pb | L | 3 | p | bb | - | A | 2 | • | |
| Tribute | 7.2 | m | dp | L | 3 | p | b | - | B | 2 | | |
| Tropicana | 8.8 | m | or | L | 3 | p | bbb | ff | A | 2 | • | • |
| Typhoon | 6.7 | m | pb | L | 3 | p | bb | fff | B | 2 | | |
| Velvet Queen | N | m | mr | L | 3 | p | b | - | B | 2 | | |
| Voodoo | N | m | ob | L | 3 | p | b | - | B | 2 | | |
| Wendy Cussons | 6.0 | m | mr | L | 3 | p | bb | fff | B | 2 | | |
| Whiskey Mac | 6.4 | m | yb | L | 3 | cu | bb | ff | B | 2 | | |
| White Masterpiece | 7.3 | m | w | L | 3 | p | bb | ff | C | 2 | | |
| Yankee Doodle | 7.2 | m | yb | L | 3 | p | bb | f | B | 2 | | |
| **FLORIBUNDA (F)** | | | | | | | | | | | | |
| Aberdonian | N | m | rb | L | 3 | cu | bbb | f | B | 2 | • | |
| Amber Queen | N | s | ab | L | 3 | p | bb | f | A | 2 | • | |
| Anabell | 8.5 | m | or | L | 3 | ca | bbb | f | B | 2 | • | • |
| Angel Face | 8.3 | s | mb | L | 3 | p | b | fff | A | 2 | • | |
| Angelina | N | t | pb | L | 1 | fl | bbb | f | B | 2 | • | |
| Anne Cocker | N | m | or | M | 3 | p | bb | - | A | 2 | • | |
| Anne Harkness | N | m | ab | M | 3 | p | bb | f | B | 2 | | |
| Arthur Bell | 7.0 | m | my | L | 2 | p | bb | fff | A | 2 | • | |
| Bahia | 7.1 | m | ob | M | 3 | cu | bb | f | A | 2 | • | |
| Betty Prior | 8.2 | m | mp | M | 1 | cu | bbb | f | A | 2 | • | |
| Bon Bon | 7.2 | s | pb | L | 2 | cu | bb | f | B | 2 | | |
| Burma Star | N | t | yb | L | 3 | cu | bbb | f | A | 2 | • | |
| Cathedral | 7.2 | m | ab | L | 3 | p | bb | f | B | 2 | | |
| Cherish | 8.0 | s | mp | L | 3 | p | bbb | f | A | 2 | • | |
| Chinatown | N | m | dy | L | 3 | cu | bb | fff | B | 2 | | |

Table 2
## SUMMARY OF ROSE CHARACTERISTICS *(Continued)*

| ROSE CLASSES and CULTIVARS | ARS RATING | HEIGHT | COLOR | BLOSSOM SIZE | BLOSSOM TYPE | BLOSSOM FORM | CONTINUITY OF BLOOM | FRAGRANCE | PERFORMANCE AT ROSE SHOWS | HARDINESS for the PRAIRIES | GEORGE'S CHOICE | THE TOP FIFTY |
|---|---|---|---|---|---|---|---|---|---|---|---|---|
| Circus | 7.0 | m | yb | M | 3 | p | bb | f | A | 2 | | |
| City of Belfast | 7.8 | m | or | M | 3 | cu | bb | - | B | 2 | | |
| Dearest | N | s | pb | L | 3 | p | bb | f | B | 2 | | |
| Elizabeth of Glamis | N | t | dp | L | 3 | fl | bbb | fff | A | 2 | • | |
| Europeana | 9.1 | m | dr | L | 3 | fl | bbb | f | A | 2 | • | • |
| Eutin | 6.9 | m | dr | S | 3 | fl | bbb | f | B | 2 | | |
| Evelyn Fisson | 7.5 | m | mr | M | 3 | cu | bbb | f | B | 2 | • | |
| Evening Star | 8.2 | m | w | M | 3 | p | bbb | f | B | 2 | • | |
| Eyepaint | 7.9 | m | rb | M | 1 | fl | bbb | f | A | 2 | • | • |
| Fashion | 7.4 | s | pb | L | 3 | fl | bbb | f | A | 2 | • | • |
| Fire King | 7.5 | m | or | M | 3 | fl | bb | f | B | 2 | | |
| First Edition | 8.4 | m | ob | M | 3 | p | b | f | A | 2 | • | |
| Fragrant Delight | N | m | ob | L | 3 | cu | bbb | fff | B | 2 | | |
| Frensham | 7.5 | m | dr | M | 2 | fl | bbb | f | B | 2 | | |
| Fresco | N | m | ob | L | 3 | p | bbb | f | A | 2 | | |
| Gene Boerner | 8.8 | m | mp | M | 3 | p | bbb | - | A | 2 | • | • |
| Ginger | 7.8 | m | or | L | 3 | cu | bb | f | B | 2 | • | |
| Glenfiddich | 6.5 | m | dy | L | 3 | p | bb | ff | B | 2 | | |
| Glengary | N | m | or | L | 3 | p | bb | - | B | 2 | | |
| Heaven Scent | N | m | pb | L | 3 | p | bb | fff | B | 2 | | |
| Iceberg | 8.9 | m | w | L | 3 | cu | bbb | fff | A | 2 | • | • |
| Impatient | 7.8 | m | or | M | 3 | ca | bb | f | A | 2 | • | |
| Intrigue | 7.2 | m | m | L | 3 | cu | b | - | B | 2 | | |
| Ivory Fashion | 8.4 | m | w | L | 2 | cu | bb | f | A | 2 | • | • |
| Korresia (Sunsprite) | 8.9 | s | dy | M | 3 | cu | bbb | fff | A | 2 | • | |
| Lavender Lassie (H Msk) | 5.0 | t | m | M | 3 | ca | bbb | fff | C | 2 | | |
| Lilli Marleen | 7.9 | m | mr | L | 3 | cu | bbb | f | A | 2 | • | |
| Little Darling | 8.8 | m | yb | M | 3 | cu | bbb | ff | A | 2 | • | • |
| Lively Lady | N | m | or | M | 3 | p | bb | f | A | 2 | • | |
| Liverpool Echo | 8.1 | m | ab | L | 3 | p | bbb | f | A | 2 | • | • |
| Margaret Merril | N | m | w | S | 3 | cu | bbb | ff | B | 2 | • | |
| Marina | 7.6 | m | ob | L | 3 | p | b | f | A | 2 | | |
| Molly McGredy | N | m | rb | L | 3 | cu | bb | f | B | 2 | | |
| Montana (Royal Occasion) | N | m | or | L | 3 | p | bbb | f | B | 2 | • | |
| Mountbatten | 7.8 | m | my | M | 3 | cu | bbb | f | A | 2 | • | |

## Table 2
## SUMMARY OF ROSE CHARACTERISTICS *(Continued)*

| ROSE CLASSES and CULTIVARS | ARS RATING | HEIGHT | COLOR | BLOSSOM SIZE | BLOSSOM TYPE | BLOSSOM FORM | CONTINUITY OF BLOOM | FRAGRANCE | PERFORMANCE AT ROSE SHOWS | HARDINESS for the PRAIRIES | GEORGE'S CHOICE | THE TOP FIFTY |
|---|---|---|---|---|---|---|---|---|---|---|---|---|
| Orangeade | 8.2 | m | or | M | 2 | cu | bb | f | A | 2 | • | |
| Paddy McGredy | 6.9 | m | mp | L | 3 | cu | bb | f | B | 2 | | |
| Pernille Poulsen | 7.5 | m | mp | L | 2 | fl | bb | f | B | 2 | | |
| Pinocchio | 7.0 | m | pb | S | 3 | cu | bb | f | B | 2 | | |
| Redgold | 7.9 | m | yb | M | 3 | p | bb | f | A | 2 | • | |
| Red Pinocchio | 7.2 | m | dr | L | 3 | cu | bb | f | B | 2 | • | |
| Regensberg | 8.1 | m | pb | L | 3 | p | bbb | f | B | 2 | • | |
| Rob Roy | N | m | dr | L | 3 | p | bbb | f | A | 2 | • | • |
| Rosa glutinosa - fragrant foliage | | s | | | | | | fff | | | | |
| Rose primula - fragrant foliage | | t | | | | | | fff | | | | |
| Rose Parade | 7.7 | m | pb | L | 3 | cu | bb | f | A | 2 | • | |
| Sarabande | 7.0 | m | or | M | 1,2 | fl | bbb | f | A | 2 | • | |
| Saratoga | 7.5 | m | w | M | 3 | cu | bb | fff | B | 2 | | |
| Sea Pearl | 8.5 | m | pb | M | 3 | p | bbb | f | A | 2 | • | • |
| Showbiz | 8.0 | s | mr | M | 3 | fl | bbb | f | B | 2 | • | |
| Simplicity | 8.3 | m | mp | L | 2 | fl | bb | f | A | 2 | • | |
| Spartan | 7.2 | m | or | L | 3 | p | bb | fff | B | 2 | • | • |
| Sue Lawley | 7.5 | m | rb | M | 2 | fl | bbb | f | A | 2 | • | |
| Sunflare | 7.8 | m | my | M | 3 | p | bb | f | B | 2 | | |
| The Sun | N | m | or | L | 2 | cu | bbb | f | B | 2 | • | |
| Tom Tom | 7.6 | m | dp | L | 3 | p | bb | f | B | 2 | | |
| Traumerei | 8.0 | m | ob | M | 3 | cu | bbb | fff | B | 2 | • | |
| Trumpeter | 8.0 | m | or | L | 3 | fl | bbb | f | B | 2 | • | |
| Viva | 7.4 | m | dr | M | 3 | p | bbb | f | B | 2 | | |
| Vogue | 7.5 | m | pb | M | 3 | p | bb | f | B | 2 | | |
| Woburn Abbey | 6.6 | s | ob | L | 3 | cu | bb | f | B | 2 | | |
| Yesterday | N | m | mp | S | 2 | fl | bbb | f | A | 2 | • | |
| **GRANDIFLORA (GR)** | | | | | | | | | | | | |
| Aquarius | 8.0 | m | pb | L | 3 | p | b | f | A | 1 | | |
| Arizona | 6.1 | m | ob | M | 3 | p | bbb | fff | B | 2 | • | |
| Ben Hur | 7.2 | m | dr | L | 3 | p | bb | f | B | 2 | | |
| Camelot | 7.7 | m | mp | L | 3 | cu | bb | f | B | 2 | | |
| Carrousel | 7.1 | m | mr | M | 3 | p | bb | f | B | 2 | | |

Table 2
## SUMMARY OF ROSE CHARACTERISTICS *(Continued)*

| ROSE CLASSES and CULTIVARS | ARS RATING | HEIGHT | COLOR | BLOSSOM SIZE | BLOSSOM TYPE | BLOSSOM FORM | CONTINUITY OF BLOOM | FRAGRANCE | PERFORMANCE AT ROSE SHOWS | HARDINESS for the PRAIRIES | GEORGE'S CHOICE | THE TOP FIFTY |
|---|---|---|---|---|---|---|---|---|---|---|---|---|
| Comanche | 6.8 | m | or | M | 3 | p | bbb | f | A | 2 | • | • |
| Dr. Eldon Lyle | 7.1 | m | dr | M | 3 | p | bb | f | B | 2 | • | |
| El Capitan | 7.8 | m | mr | L | 3 | p | bb | f | A | 2 | • | |
| Expo '86 | N | m | or | L | 3 | p | b | - | - | 2 | | |
| Flamingo Queen | N | m | mp | L | 3 | p | bbb | f | B | 2 | • | • |
| Golden Girl | 6.2 | m | my | L | 3 | p | bb | f | B | 2 | | |
| John S. Armstrong | 7.4 | m | dr | L | 3 | cu | bb | f | B | 2 | | |
| Love | 7.3 | m | rb | M | 3 | p | bbb | - | B | 2 | • | |
| Montezuma | 7.1 | t | or | L | 3 | p | bb | f | A | 2 | | |
| Mount Shasta | 7.3 | t | w | L | 3 | cu | bbb | f | A | 2 | • | • |
| New Year | N | s | ob | L | 3 | p | bb | f | A | 2 | | |
| Olé | 7.9 | t | or | M | 3 | p | bbb | f | A | 2 | • | • |
| Pink Parfait | 8.7 | m | pb | L | 3 | cu | bbb | f | A | 2 | • | • |
| Prima Donna | N | m | dp | L | 3 | p | - | f | - | 2 | • | |
| Prominent | 7.2 | m | or | L | 3 | cu | bb | f | A | 2 | • | |
| Queen Elizabeth | 9.1 | t | mp | L | 3 | p | bbb | f | A | 2 | • | • |
| Roundelay | 7.6 | m | dr | L | 3 | fl | bb | f | B | 2 | • | |
| San Antonio | 6.9 | m | or | L | 3 | p | bb | - | B | 2 | | |
| Scarlet Knight | 7.4 | m | mr | L | 3 | cu | bbb | f | B | 2 | • | |
| Shreveport | 7.4 | m | ob | L | 3 | p | b | f | B | 1 | | |
| Sonia | 8.1 | m | pb | M | 3 | p | bbb | fff | A | 2 | • | • |
| Sundowner | 7.0 | m | ab | L | 3 | p | b | fff | A | 2 | | |
| White Lightnin' | 7.4 | m | w | L | 3 | p | bbb | f | A | 2 | • | |
| **POLYANTHA** (Pol) | | | | | | | | | | | | |
| Cameo | 7.6 | s | mp | S | 3 | cu | bb | f | A | 2 | • | |
| Cecile Brunner | 8.0 | m | lp | S | 3 | p | bbb | f | A | 2 | • | • |
| China Doll | 8.2 | s | mp | S | 3 | cu | bbb | f | A | 2 | • | |
| Dick Koster | 7.8 | s | dp | S | 3 | cu | bbb | - | B | 2 | | |
| Dopey | N | s | mr | S | 2 | cu | bbb | - | B | 2 | | |
| Ideal | 6.6 | s | mr | S | 3 | cu | bb | f | B | 2 | | |
| Lullaby | N | m | w | S | 3 | fl | bbb | f | A | 2 | • | |
| Margo Koster | 7.6 | s | ob | S | 3 | cu | bbb | f | B | 2 | | |
| Mothersday | 7.1 | s | dr | S | 3 | cu | bbb | - | A | 2 | • | |
| Snow White | N | s | w | S | 3 | cu | bb | - | B | 2 | | |

Table 2
## SUMMARY OF ROSE CHARACTERISTICS *(Continued)*

| ROSE CLASSES and CULTIVARS | ARS RATING | HEIGHT | COLOR | BLOSSOM SIZE | BLOSSOM TYPE | BLOSSOM FORM | CONTINUITY OF BLOOM | FRAGRANCE | PERFORMANCE AT ROSE SHOWS | HARDINESS for the PRAIRIES | GEORGE'S CHOICE | THE TOP FIFTY |
|---|---|---|---|---|---|---|---|---|---|---|---|---|
| Sparkler | 7.5 | s | mr | S | 2 | cu | bbb | - | A | 2 | | |
| The Fairy | 8.7 | s | lp | S | 3 | fl | bb | - | A | 2 | • | • |
| Verdun | N | s | mr | S | 3 | cu | bb | - | B | 2 | | |
| **CLIMBER  (Cl)** | | | | | | | | | | | | |
| Blaze | 7.8 | t | mr | M | 2 | cu | bbb | f | A | 2 | • | |
| Danse du Feu (Spectacular) | N | t | or | M | 3 | fl | bbb | - | A | 2 | • | |
| Maigold | 6.0 | t | dy | L | 2 | cu | b | fff | B | 2 | • | |
| Morning Jewel | 6.5 | t | mp | L | 2 | cu | bbb | f | A | 2 | • | |
| Rosarium Uetersen | 8.0 | t | dp | M | 3 | fl | bbb | f | A | 2 | • | |
| **MINIATURE   (Min)** | | | | | | | | | | | | |
| Angel Darling | 7.8 | s | m | S | 1 | fl | bbb | f | B | 2 | | |
| Baby Cecile Brunner | 8.0 | s | lp | S | 3 | p | bb | f | A | 2 | | |
| Baby Masquerade | 7.2 | s | rb | S | 3 | fl | bbb | f | B | 2 | | |
| Beauty Secret | 9.3 | s | mr | S | 3 | p | bbb | fff | A | 2 | • | |
| Cupcake | 8.6 | s | mp | S | 3 | cu | bbb | f | A | 2 | • | |
| Dilly Dilly | 7.6 | s | m | S | 3 | p | bbb | - | A | 2 | • | |
| Dreamglo | 8.5 | s | rb | S | 3 | p | bbb | f | A | 2 | | |
| Fresh Pink | 8.2 | s | lp | S | 3 | cu | bbb | f | A | 2 | | |
| Golden Song (Cl) | 7.6 | s | yb | S | 3 | fl | bb | - | A | 2 | | |
| Green Ice | 7.6 | s | w | S | 3 | cu | bb | - | A | 2 | | |
| Hi Ho (Cl) | 8.6 | s | dp | S | 3 | cu | bbb | - | A | 2 | | |
| Holy Toledo | 8.5 | s | ab | S | 3 | ca | bbb | - | A | 2 | | |
| Hula Girl | 7.5 | s | ob | S | 3 | p | bb | f | A | 2 | | |
| Jeanne Lajoie (Cl) | 8.6 | s | mp | S | 3 | p | bbb | f | A | 2 | • | |
| Judy Fischer | 8.6 | s | mp | S | 3 | p | bbb | f | A | 2 | • | |
| Lavender Jewel | 8.1 | s | m | S | 3 | p | bbb | f | A | 2 | • | |
| Lemon Delight | 7.0 | s | my | S | 2 | fl | bbb | f | B | 2 | | |
| Little Eskimo | 8.3 | s | w | S | 3 | p | bbb | - | A | 2 | • | |
| Magic Carrousel | 9.3 | s | rb | S | 3 | p | bbb | f | A | 2 | | |
| Minnie Pearl | 8.1 | s | pb | S | 3 | p | bb | f | A | 2 | | |

Table 2
## SUMMARY OF ROSE CHARACTERISTICS *(Continued)*

| ROSE CLASSES and CULTIVARS | ARS RATING | HEIGHT | COLOR | BLOSSOM SIZE | BLOSSOM TYPE | BLOSSOM FORM | CONTINUITY OF BLOOM | FRAGRANCE | PERFORMANCE AT ROSE SHOWS | HARDINESS for the PRAIRIES | GEORGE'S CHOICE | THE TOP FIFTY |
|---|---|---|---|---|---|---|---|---|---|---|---|---|
| Orange Cascade (Cl) | 7.0 | s | ob | S | 3 | fl | bb | f | A | 2 | | |
| Over the Rainbow | 8.5 | s | rb | S | 3 | p | bbb | f | A | 2 | | |
| Over the Rainbow (Cl) | 8.0 | s | rb | S | 3 | p | bbb | f | A | 2 | | |
| Peaches 'n' Cream | 8.6 | s | pb | S | 3 | p | bbb | f | A | 2 | | |
| Popcorn | 8.2 | s | w | S | 2 | fl | bbb | f | A | 2 | • | |
| Red Cascade (Cl) | 7.5 | s | dr | S | 3 | cu | bbb | f | A | 2 | • | |
| Rise 'n' Shine | 9.0 | s | my | S | 3 | p | bbb | f | A | 2 | • | |
| Scarlet Gem | 7.6 | s | or | S | 3 | cu | bbb | f | A | 2 | • | • |
| Sheri Anne | 8.6 | s | or | S | 2 | fl | bbb | f | A | 2 | • | |
| Starina | 9.6 | s | or | S | 3 | fl | bbb | - | A | 2 | • | |
| Top Secret | 8.6 | s | mr | S | 3 | p | bbb | f | A | 2 | • | |
| Toy Clown | 8.6 | s | rb | S | 2 | ca | bbb | - | A | 2 | • | |
| White Angel | 8.4 | s | w | S | 3 | p | bbb | f | A | 2 | • | |
| Yellow Doll (Cl) | 7.5 | s | my | S | 3 | p | bbb | f | A | 2 | | |
| **RUGOSA, SHRUB and SHRUB TYPE** | | | | | | | | | | | | |
| Adelaide Hoodless | N | t | mr | M | 2 | fl | bbb | f | A | 4 | • | • |
| Altaica | - | t | my | M | 1 | fl | b | f | - | 4 | • | |
| Assiniboine (H Suf) | N | t | mr | M | 2 | fl | bb | f | - | 4 | | |
| Austrian Copper | 8.0 | t | rb | M | 1 | fl | bb | ff | - | 4 | | |
| Betty Bland | 6.5 | t | dp | M | 3 | fl | b | f | - | 4 | | |
| Blanc de Coubert (H RG) | 8.0 | t | w | L | 3 | cu | bb | fff | - | 3 | | |
| Bonica (S) | N | m | mp | M | 3 | cu | bbb | f | B | 2 | • | |
| Carmenetta (red foliage) | 5.8 | t | lp | S | 1 | cu | bbb | f | - | 4 | | |
| Champlain | N | m | dr | M | 3 | cu | bbb | f | - | 4 | | |
| Charles Albanel (H Rg) | N | s | mr | M | 3 | cu | bb | ff | - | 4 | | |
| Cuthbert Grant (H Suf) | N | m | dr | L | 3 | cu | bb | f | B | 4 | • | • |
| David Thompson (H Rg) | N | m | mr | M | 3 | fl | bbb | ff | B | 4 | • | |
| George Will (H Rg) | N | m | dp | M | 3 | fl | bbb | ff | B | 4 | • | |
| Grootendorst Supreme (H Rg) | 7.7 | m | dr | S | 3 | fl | bbb | - | B | 4 | • | |
| Hansa (H Rg) | 8.5 | t | mr | L | 3 | fl | bbb | ff | B | 4 | • | • |

Table 2
## SUMMARY OF ROSE CHARACTERISTICS *(Continued)*

| ROSE CLASSES and CULTIVARS | ARS RATING | HEIGHT | COLOR | BLOSSOM SIZE | BLOSSOM TYPE | BLOSSOM FORM | CONTINUITY OF BLOOM | FRAGRANCE | PERFORMANCE AT ROSE SHOWS | HARDINESS for the PRAIRIES | GEORGE'S CHOICE | THE TOP FIFTY |
|---|---|---|---|---|---|---|---|---|---|---|---|---|
| Harrison's Yellow (H Ft) | 7.6 | t | dy | S | 2 | fl | b | fff | B | 4 | • | |
| Helen Bland (thornless) | - | t | dp | M | 2 | fl | b | f | - | 4 | | |
| Henry Hudson (H Rg) | N | s | w | M | 3 | f | bb | f | - | 4 | | |
| Isabella Skinner | N | t | mp | M | 3 | cu | bb | - | - | 4 | • | |
| Jens Munk (H Rg) | N | m | mp | M | 3 | fl | bbb | f | B | 4 | | |
| John Cabot | N | t | mr | M | 3 | cu | bbb | f | B | 4 | | |
| Marie Bugnet | - | m | w | M | 3 | fl | bbb | fff | B | 4 | | |
| Martin Frobisher | N | t | lp | M | 3 | fl | bb | ff | - | 4 | | |
| Morden Amorette | N | s | dp | M | 3 | cu | bb | - | - | 4 | | |
| Morden Cardinette | N | s | mr | M | 3 | cu | bb | f | - | 4 | | |
| Morden Centennial | N | s | mp | M | 3 | fl | bb | f | - | 4 | | |
| Morden Ruby | N | s | pb | M | 3 | fl | bb | f | - | 4 | | |
| Nova Zembla (H Rg) | 7.1 | t | w | L | 3 | cu | b | f | - | 4 | | |
| Persian Yellow (H Ft) | - | t | my | S | 2 | cu | b | - | - | 4 | • | |
| Pink Grootendorst (H Rg) | 8.6 | m | p | S | 3 | fl | bbb | - | B | 4 | • | |
| Prairie Dawn | 6.4 | t | mp | M | 3 | fl | bbb | f | B | 4 | • | • |
| Red Grootendorst (H Rg) | - | m | mr | S | 3 | fl | bbb | - | B | 4 | | • |
| Therese Bugnet (H Rg) | 7.8 | t | dp | L | 3 | fl | bbb | f | B | 4 | • | • |
| Wasagaming (H Rg) | N | m | mp | L | 3 | fl | bb | f | - | 4 | | |

Table 2
## SUMMARY OF ROSE CHARACTERISTICS - LEGEND

ARS Rating: American Rose Society Rating. 10 indicates a perfect score; 7 a good one; 5 mediocre; 2 poor; N - a new rose or one recently introduced to North America and worthy of trial.

HEIGHT:
s - short, under 60 cm (2 ft.)
m - medium, 60 to 90 cm (2 to 3 ft.)
t - tall, over 90 cm (3 ft.)

COLOR: ab - apricot blend; dr - dark red; dp - deep pink; dy - dark yellow; lp - light pink; m - mauve; mr - medium red; my - medium yellow; o - orange; or - orange red; pb - pink blend; r - russet; rb - red blend; w - white; y - yellow; yb - yellow blend

BLOSSOM SIZE:
(S) - small, under 5 cm (2 in.) in diameter
(M) - medium, 5 to 10 cm ( 2 to 4 in.)
(L) - large, over 10 cm (4 in.)

BLOSSOM TYPE:
(1) single - up to 12 petals
(2) semi-double - 13 - 20 petals
(3) double - over 20 petals
This is the most commonly accepted standard for bloom type. However, you may, on occasion, hear some rosarians who differ on how many petals a single or semi-double type of bloom should have. Some rosarians classify a single as not more than 8 petals and a semi-double as 9 - 20 petals.

BLOSSOM FORM:
p - Pointed and high centered. Most people recognize this as a classic shape for a rose, a feature that is highly esteemed. Christian Dior, Korde's Perfecta, and Pascali are good examples.
cu - Cupped. The shape of the blossom is like a cup in profile. Gypsy, Mothersday, and Margo Koster are examples of this form.
ca - Camellia-like. The petals are bent back over each other like a camellia, as in Prominent.
fl - Flat. The flower is shallow with petals growing out at nearly right angles from the base of the flower. Altai and Sterling Silver exhibit this characteristic.
ru - Ruffled petals giving the flower an irregular outline. Aberdonian and some of the old species roses have this form.

CONTINUITY OF BLOOM:
bbb - blooms freely and abundantly.
bb - moderate in bloom production.
b - somewhat "stingy" with bloom production and bloom repeat or non-recurrent.

FRAGRANCE:
fff - very fragrant
ff - medium fragrance
f - slight fragrance

PERFORMANCE AT ROSE SHOWS:
A - has won top honors at many rose shows.
B - has occasionally won top awards.
C - has seldom won at rose shows.

Table 2
## SUMMARY OF ROSE CHARACTERISTICS - LEGEND (*Continued*)

| | |
|---|---|
| HARDINESS FOR THE PRAIRIES: | 1 - only occasionally survives with protection suggested in this book.<br>2 - requires complete protection as outlined in this book.<br>3 - requires less protection and occasionally survives with little or no protection for winter.<br>4 - survives most winters without any special protective measures. |
| GEORGE'S CHOICE: | • - from the author's rose growing experience, he recommends it as a good reliable cultivar. |
| ROSE CLASSES: | HT - Hybrid Tea; HP - Hybrid Perpetual; HRg - Hybrid Rugosa; HFt - Hybrid Foetida; HMsk - Hybrid Musk; HSuf - Hybrid Suffulta; S - shrub; Sp - species (old Garden Rose); Gr - Grandiflora; F - Floribunda; Pol - Polyantha; Min - Miniature; Cl - Climber |

Table 2
## SUMMARY OF ROSE CHARACTERISTICS - TOP FIFTY

**HYBRID TEA**

AVE MARIA ( HT)

BEL ANGE (HT)

BURGUND '81 (LOVING MEMORY) (HT)

CHICAGO PEACE (HT)

CHRYSLER IMPERIAL (HT)

DOUBLE DELIGHT (HT)

DUET (HT)

ELECTRON (HT)

GARDEN PARTY (HT)

Table 2
## SUMMARY OF ROSE CHARACTERISTICS - TOP FIFTY *(Continued)*

GOLDEN JUBILEE (HT)　　LOLITA (HT)　　MISS ALL AMERICAN BEAUTY (HT)

MISTER LINCOLN (HT)　　ORIANA (HT)　　PASCALI (HT)

PEACE (HT)　　PETER FRANKENFELD (HT)　　PORTRAIT (HT)

Table 2
SUMMARY OF ROSE CHARACTERISTICS - TOP FIFTY (Continued)

QUEEN O' THE LAKES  (HT)

RED QUEEN  (HT)

ROYAL DANE (TROIKA)  (HT)

SILVER STAR  (HT)

TROPICANA  (HT)

**FLORIBUNDA**

ANABELL  (F)

EUROPEANA  (F)

EYEPAINT  (F)

## Table 2
## SUMMARY OF ROSE CHARACTERISTICS - TOP FIFTY *(Continued)*

FASHION (F)

GENE BOERNER (F)

ICEBERG (F)

IVORY FASHION (F)

LITTLE DARLING (F)

LIVERPOOL ECHO (F)

ROB ROY (F)

SEA PEARL (F)

SUE LAWLEY (F)

Table 1
## SUMMARY OF ROSE CHARACTERISTICS - TOP FIFTY *(Continued)*

**GRANDIFLORA**

| | | |
|---|---|---|
| COMANCHE (Gr) | FLAMINGO QUEEN (Gr) | MOUNT SHASTA (Gr) |
| OLÉ (Gr) | PINK PARFAIT (Gr) | QUEEN ELIZABETH (Gr) |
| SONIA (Gr) | **POLYANTHA** CECILE BRUNNER (Pol) | THE FAIRY (Pol) |

Table 2
SUMMARY OF ROSE CHARACTERISTICS - TOP FIFTY *(Continued)*

**MINIATURE**
SCARLET GEM (Min)

**RUGOSA/SHRUB/SHRUB TYPE**
ADELAIDE HOODLESS (S)

CUTHBERT GRANT (H Suf)

HANSA (H Rg)

PRAIRIE DAWN (S)

THERESE BUGNET (H Rg)

# PLANNING THE ROSE GARDEN

All landscapers advise you to plan before you plant. It is easier to change the plan than to dig and re-plant at a later date. Although roses make up only a small portion of the total home landscape, they should fit and add interest and beauty to the complete plan.

## PAPER AND PENCIL PLANNING

A garden plan is just as important as a house plan (see Figure 9, GARDEN PLAN). The garden and the home are part of each other and should be thought of as a complete unit. If well planned, a very pleasant living area is created.

In order to properly proportion the areas for plantings, it is necessary to have a plan drawn to scale. If you draw several plans, you can choose and integrate the best aspects of each. Try to involve all the members of the household in determining the basic requirements of the garden.

Take the following steps when you plan your rose garden:
1. Consider your budget.
2. Choose the size, shape, and location of the rose bed or beds.
3. Examine soil conditions, drainage, water, shelter, and other aspects of plant care.
4. Select the number of roses of each kind (class), variety, and color needed.
5. Choose a supplier to purchase your roses from.
6. Plan for the storage of equipment and materials needed to maintain the garden.

This manual cannot cover all aspects of planning a garden. Each garden plan must be geared to the individual needs and wishes of the occupants.

## LOCATION AND EXPOSURE

Good shelter to the west and north of the rose beds should be provided to protect them from strong winds and at times the rains that often accompany such weather. A tall, solid board or picket fence makes a good shelter. Tree and hedge shelters provide better protection, but you must be certain that tree roots do not interfere with the rose bed. Roses should be kept 4.5 - 6.0 m (15 - 20 ft.) away from large trees like spruce, ash, elm, or Manitoba maple. Also beware of poplars: Northwest, Russian, Griffin, native Black Poplar or Balm-of-Gilead, and the native White Poplar or Trembling Aspen. All of these trees have tremendously long and shallow roots that are likely to invade your rose bed even from as far as 10 - 15 m (30 - 50 ft.).

In most gardens it is difficult to locate rose beds a safe distance from large trees on the property. In such cases a barrier between the trees and the rose bed can be installed (see Figure 8, ROOT BARRIER). This can be achieved by digging a trench 60 cm (2 ft.) deep and installing heavy gauge galvanized tin, standing on edge to the surface level. Overlap pieces 8 - 10 cm (3 - 4 in.) and caulk the ends. A crack or hole in the barrier is sure to be found by tree roots. Refill the trench and the barrier will not be noticeable. Suitable substitutes for galvanized tin are heavy fibreglass sheets or 12 mil polyethylene.

Roses cannot be grown in shade; they require sunlight for at least eight hours per day. Less than this will result in weak, spindly, and unproductive rose bushes.

Figure 8
ROOT BARRIER

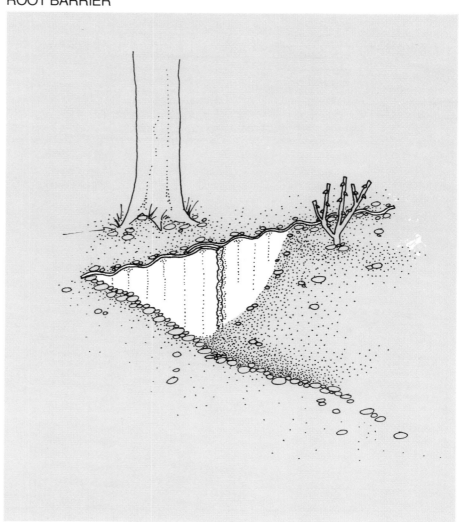

Figure 9
GARDEN PLAN

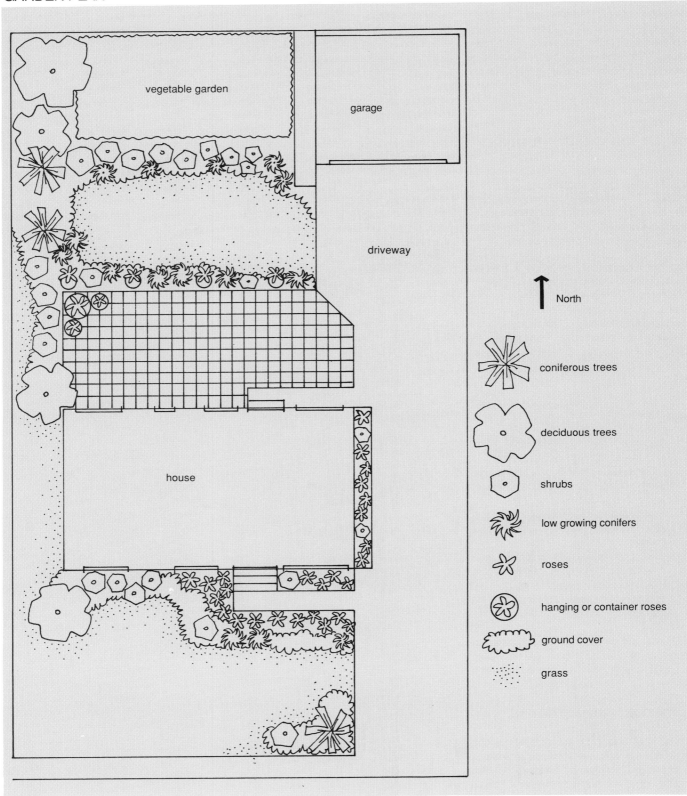

## Figure 10
## SHEWCHUK RESIDENCE

garage

patio

house

driveway

North ←

coniferous trees

deciduous trees

shrubs

low growing conifers

roses

ground cover

grass

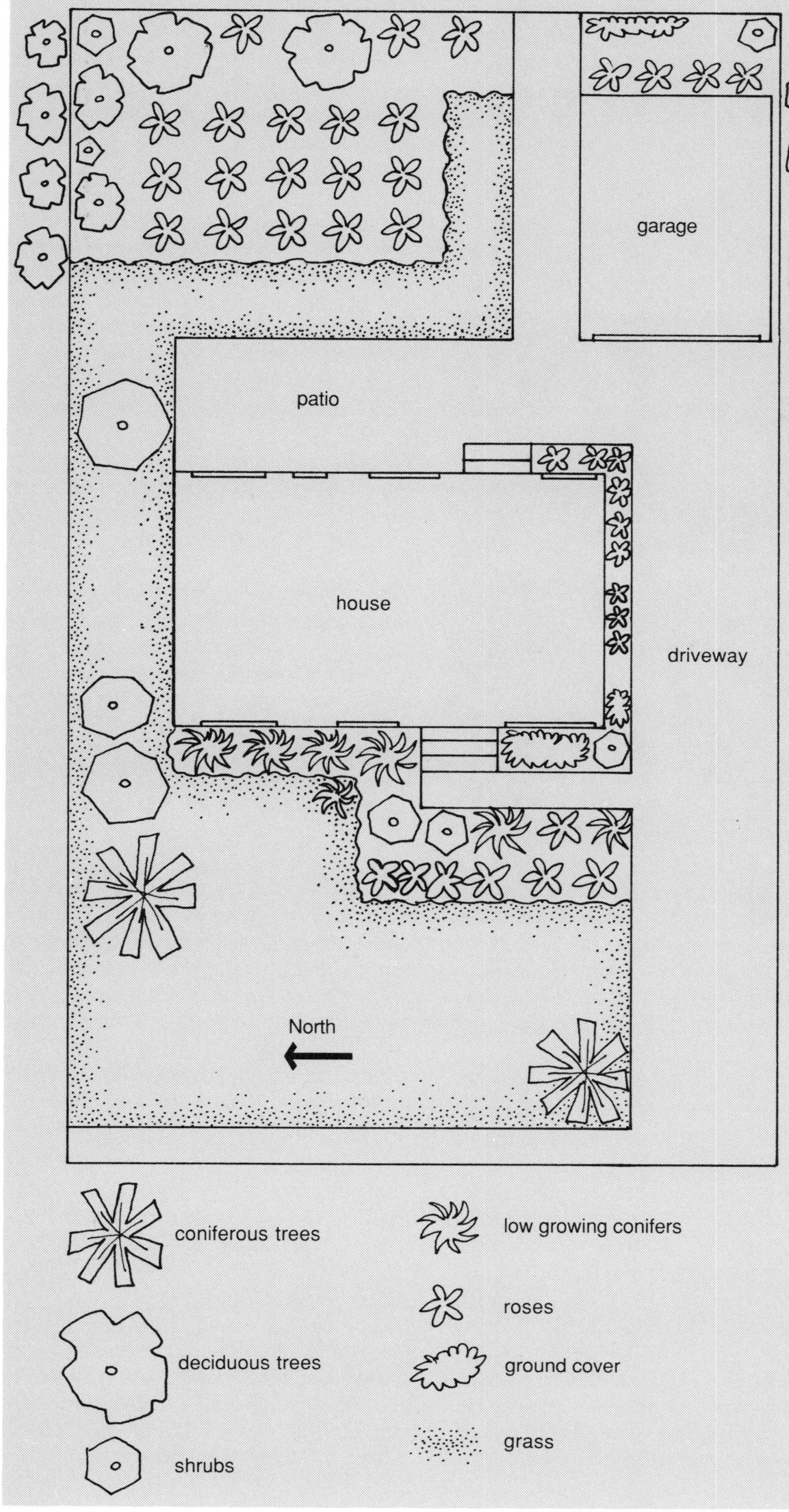

*ROSE GARDENING AT THE SHEWCHUK RESIDENCE*
*by G.W. Shewchuk*

*For purposes of illustration, let's review some of the problems the author has to deal with (see Figure 10, SHEWCHUK RESIDENCE). We have a large rose bed on the east side of our house with good wind protection. The roses get sunlight for a bit more than 12 hours per day, but are bothered by tree roots from the neighbor's Black Poplar and Birch, my apple tree, a Linden, and a Burr Oak (see Figure 11, THE SHEWCHUK ROSE GARDEN).*

*Roses on the south side of our house in a narrow bed between the house and the concrete driveway, get a full day's sunlight. Protection from inclement weather is adequate but the heat from the sun is much greater than in beds in more open areas. This bed requires watering twice as often as the others. Because of the extra heat they receive, this is where I find the first appearance of spider mite infestation. In winter when we get mild spells and again in early spring, it is difficult to maintain snow cover in this location.*

*In spite of the problems we have with roses on the south side of the house, we are rewarded by getting blossoms one or two weeks earlier than from the beds in other locations. In the fall, these roses are still in bloom two to three weeks after the frost has nipped the other beds. Taking these extra two week periods together we get an additional month of blooming. The bonus of an extra month is tremendously appreciated in the short growing season on the Prairies.*

*Our third rose bed is a fairly long one on the west side of the house, about 3 m (10 ft.) away. This bed came out of a portion of our front lawn. All available space at the back of our house was taken up with roses and it became impossible to find space to plant some of the good roses we saw and heard of, or the new ones that were introduced each year. It was difficult to resist planting some beautiful rose that I did not already have. That is how our front lawn keeps getting smaller and the rose beds larger.*

*In our front bed the roses get sunlight for approximately 11 hours per day, which is more than sufficient. They also take the brunt of most of the storms that nature thrusts upon them. On a couple of occasions my wife and I have watched these roses take a terrific beating in a wind storm. The taller canes were thrashed about, leaves shredded, and flowers strewn across the garden. We have repeatedly discovered, to our pleasant surprise, the amazing ability that roses have to recover. Three or four days after the storm, all appeared normal and you would never have guessed what they had gone through.*

Figure 11
THE SHEWCHUK ROSE GARDEN

It is recommended that you protect your rose beds with a lattice work, board fence, or tree shelter. However, if this is not possible or practical, do not deprive yourself of an abundance of beautiful roses. Plant roses regardless of the risk.

### COLOR IN ROSE BEDS

Many people prefer to grow roses in formal plantings using only one cultivar or color in each bed to give a breathtaking splash of color. Each cultivar has its own bloom cycle and if a bed contains only a single cultivar and color, there will be a flowerless period before another flush of bloom appears. Other gardeners prefer mixed cultivars in each bed to get away from the "barren look" between blooming periods. Another alternative for very color conscious individuals is to group different cultivar and types of roses of similar color. This will give the desired color and a long continuous period of bloom. However, for this system to work, the rose grower must know rose cultivars and types very well.

You can create any color combination you wish, but in small areas and small beds, mixed colors lose their effectiveness. It is best to group three to five bushes of the same cultivar and color together. In larger areas, mixed colors present a riot of color.

## SOIL AND ROSES

Roses generally grow well in any soil that produces good vegetables. Roses also grow under a great variety of undesirable soil types and conditions. However, they cannot tolerate poor drainage, or unduly alkaline or acid soil.

### DRAINAGE

Adequate drainage is of vital importance to rose growing. Roses require soil that is absorbent enough to retain adequate moisture for vigorous growth, but they do not like wet feet.

Avoid planting roses in areas where water from rain and snow melt is likely to accumulate. In areas of poor drainage, raised beds may be the answer. If this is insufficient, then the installation of drainage tile may be the only solution.

### TEXTURE

Friable sandy, clay loam is just right for roses. It has the capability of draining away excess water and still retaining sufficient moisture for good plant growth.

This soil texture has a fair amount of clay with enough organic matter and coarse sand in the right proportions to make an absorbent, friable soil that crumbles easily and does not pack or dry like cement. A handful of this soil, when slightly moist and compressed, falls apart when you open your hand. You cannot make soil balls with good garden soil.

Heavy clay can be made workable and more productive by the incorporation of coarse sand, vermiculite, perlite, or organic matter. The organic matter can be in the form of well rotted cow manure, peat moss, or compost. Coarse sand should look like cracked wheat. The addition of fine sand will make such soil as hard as an adobe brick when dry.

Very sandy soil can be improved by incorporating some clay and organic matter.

### SOIL REACTION

Most home gardeners are familiar with using commercial fertilizers to improve soil fertility. However, very few are familiar with the pH factor, and how it affects soils and plant growth.

Roses do best in a soil with a pH reading of 6.0 - 6.5. This is slightly acidic. A neutral soil would have a pH reading of 7.0. Alkaline soil would have a pH higher than 7.0. For the purpose of comparision, the pH value of some common household substances are listed below:

- Pure lemon juice          2.0
- Vinegar          2.2
- Tomatoes          4.2
- Milk          6.6
- Baking soda          8.2
- Milk of magnesia          10.5
- Pure alkali (lye)          14.0

Although roses will tolerate a wider pH range than 6.0 - 6.5, it is best to provide them with optimum conditions. Roses subjected to undesirable pH levels are likely to suffer nutritional problems. The pH can be determined by using a soil test kit available from most garden supply shops or by sending samples to a Soil Testing Laboratory. If you request it, a complete analysis of your soil can be carried out showing available nitrogen, phosphorus, and potassium, plus micronutrients and special factors such as pH and salinity.

A gardener can change the pH reading of garden soil to any desired acidic or alkaline level. The addition of lime will raise the pH level; powdered sulfur will lower the pH. Powdered sulfur applied at the rate of 0.5 kg/10 m$^2$ (1.0 lb./100 sq. ft.) will lower the pH by one unit in the top 15 cm (6 in.) of soil if worked to that depth. If your soil is too acidic, the pH can be raised (sweetened) by incorporating lime at the rate of 250 g/m$^2$ (1.0 lb./ 20 sq. ft.), provided the lime is 99 percent pure. More lime will be required if it is not pure. These amounts are calculated on the basis of changing the pH one point in average sandy loam soil when incorporated to a depth of 15 cm (6 in.). To change the pH one point to a depth of 30 cm (1 ft.), it is necessary to double the amount of sulfur or lime and incorporate to a full depth of 30 cm (1 ft.).

In a few years your soil pH reading may return to its previous level due to leaching. Therefore, you need to check the acidity every year or two, and determine whether your soil pH factor needs adjusting.

Instructions given above for changing the pH of the soil refer to good friable garden loam. Soil with a more than average organic matter content will require 25 - 30 percent more amendment (sulfur or lime) for the specified area. Soil that is more sandy than the average soil will require 25 - 30 percent less amendment.

Where only a few rose bushes are involved and there is a high soil pH reading, magnesium sulfate can be used on each individual plant. This acidifier can be obtained at most garden shops. The container generally has instructions for its use.

Conversely, if the soil pH is lower than 6, adding slaked lime in the area of the plant will raise the pH. Exercise caution and don't overdo a good thing. It is best to treat lightly, test, and re-treat if necessary.

## PREPARING ROSES FOR PLANTING

Whether you receive your roses from a mail order supplier or purchase them

Figure 12
SOAKING ROSES BEFORE PLANTING

Figure 13
HEELING IN

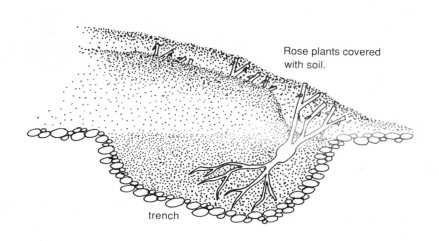

Rose plants covered with soil.

trench

from a local garden center, there are certain steps that should be taken to get your roses off to a good start.

## BASIC CARE

The first step in preparing your roses for planting is to soak their roots in water, or a solution of two tablespoons 20-20-20 fertilizer per 25 L (5 gal.) water, for one or two days (see Figure 12, SOAKING ROSES BEFORE PLANTING). You should never allow 'bare root' roses to remain packed for more than a day or two even if **you** are not ready to plant them or the weather is not co-operating.

## HEELING IN

If the rose plants you ordered arrive before you are ready, or the weather does not permit planting, they can be stored safely for up to two weeks by using the following procedure (see Figure 13, HEELING IN):

1. Dig a trench 60 cm (2 ft.) deep in a shady sheltered place.
2. Spread the rose plants out in the trench after they have received a good soaking (see BASIC CARE).
3. Lay them out at a 45 degree angle and then cover with moist soil. Leave the top quarter of the canes showing above ground.
4. Water them well.

Should there be a threat of frost, protect the tops with a burlap sacking, straw, or some other light covering.

## COLD STORAGE

A root cellar or cold storage room is also a good place to store boxed or packaged rose bushes. However, make sure that they have adequate moisture. If the packing material is dry, add water.

# PLANTING NEW PLANTS

There is more to planting roses than just digging a hole, sticking a rose plant into it, and covering the roots with soil. In this section you will discover some of the most important steps to be taken to ensure the survival of your rose plants through winter and into spring.

## Figure 14
## RECOMMENDED PLANTING METHOD

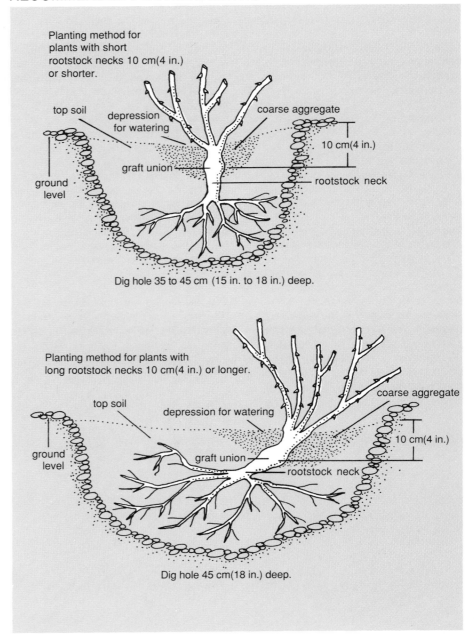

Planting method for plants with short rootstock necks 10 cm (4 in.) or shorter.

top soil — depression for watering — coarse aggregate — graft union — ground level — rootstock neck — 10 cm (4 in.)

Dig hole 35 to 45 cm (15 in. to 18 in.) deep.

Planting method for plants with long rootstock necks 10 cm (4 in.) or longer.

top soil — depression for watering — coarse aggregate — ground level — graft union — rootstock neck — 10 cm (4 in.)

Dig hole 45 cm (18 in.) deep.

## TIMING

The best time to plant roses in the average year on the Canadian Prairies is between April 25 and May 15. Quite often during this period it is windy, hot and dry; this is not very conducive to the establishment of tender plants. Plant in the late afternoon, and be prepared to give the new plants the opportunity to regain some of the energy lost through

digging, shipping, and exposure. In general, it is desirable to plant as early in the spring as possible.

## PLANTING METHOD

Planting properly has different meanings in various parts of the U.S.A. or Canada. This is obvious when the planting instructions are read on packaged roses from different parts of the continent. The uncertainty is not at all reduced by reading the numerous manuals on the market.

**In the cool agricultural areas of the Prairies, the planting method described here is the secret to successful growing of Hybrid Tea, Grandiflora, Polyantha, and Floribunda roses.** Apply the following procedures and savor the splendor of beautiful, vigorous roses.

Dig holes at least 45 cm (18 in.) deep. Replace the soil, if poor, with a rich garden loam or with a mixture of:
- one part peat moss
- one part perlite, vermiculite or coarse sand
- one part garden soil.

The addition of 1 cup of bonemeal per plant is also beneficial.

When the hole is dug and the fill soil is prepared, place a small board or cane across the middle of the hole to mark the surface level. Spread out the roots and position the plant so that the graft union is 10 cm (4 in.) below the marker. Hold the pre-soaked rose in this position as the hole is filled. Firm the soil around the roots. In the planting illustration (see Figure 14, RECOMMENDED PLANTING METHOD), note the position and depth. If you are planting packaged or boxed roses with their normally amputated roots, there is little problem positioning the roots during planting. Bushes with such very short root stocks make planting in a vertical position appropriate. The graft union is readily positioned at the 10 cm (4 in.) depth.

Under normal conditions, rose roots penetrate to a depth of 45 cm (18 in.); the majority of the roots are concentrated in the 15 - 30 cm (6 - 12 in.) soil depth zone. Plants react negatively to being planted too deep or too shallow. Long rooted bushes may need the canes and roots positioned at a 45 degree angle in order to have the majority of roots concentrated between 15 - 30 cm (6 - 12 in.) in depth, and the graft union at 10 cm (4 in.). This is shown in the illustrations on RECOMMENDED PLANTING METHOD, Figure 14. When new shoots appear, they will assume the

normal vertical position and the old angled stems will not be noticeable.

You will notice in the RECOMMENDED PLANTING METHOD illustration that, after covering the roots, coarse aggregate (coarse sand, perlite, or vermiculite) is heaped over the graft union. This is done specifically to assist new shoots from the graft union and the canes underground to easily penetrate the soil. In the event that all top growth is killed, the most vital parts of the rose plant can still send up shoots through this coarse material without too much difficulty. You will also note that after a "saucer-like" depression is made around each plant for easy watering, the graft is actually 5 cm (2 in.) below the depression surface and 10 cm (4 in.) below surface level. Immediately after planting give the rose bushes a thorough, deep soaking.

Allow plenty of room around each rose. Plant Hybrid Teas, Grandifloras and Floribundas about 60 - 75 cm (2 - 2.5 ft.) apart. For miniatures, half that distance is sufficient.

After planting and watering, cover the bushes with burlap sacking for a week to ten days. Uncover only when it is raining, or when very calm and cloudy. Under such cover the sprouts green up and harden-off to withstand the sun and drying wind. Some people hill up newly planted roses to the tips of the canes and achieve the same thing. Hilling can also be done using mulch or other insulating material. The mulching material is gradually removed when new shoots begin to show through.

Have some type of mulching material handy in the event of freezing temperatures. Burlap sacks or newspapers are also good for this purpose.

## PLANTING A POTTED ROSE BUSH

To plant a potted rose bush, dig a hole twice the diameter and twice the depth of the pot. Then remove the plant from the pot. Roses purchased in tapered plastic pots slip out very easily if the soil is a bit dry. If this is not the case, cut through

the pot in two or three places without disturbing the roots. Tear away the pot, and remove the root ball. Metal pots are more difficult to handle, but can be cut with a good set of tinsmith shears. Partially fill the hole with good soil, making certain that when the unpotted plant is set in the hole, the graft union will be 10 cm (4 in.) below ground level. Now fill the rest of the hole around the root ball with good soil. Firm up the soil and form a shallow dish 5 cm (2 in.) deep around the rose canes. Fill with water several times to thoroughly soak the soil.

## PLANTING MINIATURE ROSES

Miniature roses are relatively easy to plant. They are not grafted or budded but grown from cuttings. Their root system is quite small in comparison to larger roses. Plant them 4 - 5 cm (1.5 - 2 in.) deeper than they were in the original containers. In all other aspects, growing miniatures is very similar to growing larger roses.

## TRANSPLANTING

Transplanting a rose in full bloom is generally not recommended, but it can be done if reasonable care and attention is exercised. The rose should be well watered the day before transplanting to help the soil adhere to the roots. The plant should be sprayed with a product such as Wilt-Pruf several hours before transplanting. Be sure that coverage of both upper and lower leaf surfaces is complete. Wilt-Pruf is a wax-like spray that protects plants from excessive transpiration.

Dig up the plant carefully to maintain as large a root ball as possible. Moving the plant is easier if the root ball is covered with burlap and tied or held firmly.

The Wilt-Pruf coating will have become gradually weathered away by the time the plant has become established. If it is extremely hot, the plant should be shaded for a couple of days. Shading can be achieved by using garden stakes 30 - 90 cm (2 - 3 ft.) long inserted in the soil and covered by a piece of burlap. If the first few days are cloudy and cool, no protection is necessary.

Figure 15
## CONTAINER GARDENING

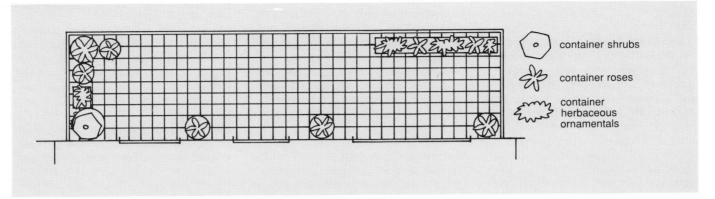

container shrubs

container roses

container
herbaceous
ornamentals

### REPLACING ROSE BUSHES

When planting new roses to replace old or failing bushes, remove 45 - 55 L (10 - 12 gal.) of soil where the old bush had grown and replace with new soil. Use the soil mixture recommended under the PLANTING METHOD section. If the old bush had root or crown gall, or any other disease, remove twice or even three times as much soil. This should provide a good base for a new rose. Be sure to burn the discarded rose. This will destroy any harbored diseases or insects.

### RENOVATING OLD ROSE BEDS

On the Prairies more trials and research are needed to determine when it is best to replace old worn-out plants. In the author's experience, most good rose cultivars remain quite productive for 10 - 12 years, although some last up to 20 years.

After a number of years, all roses gradually fade away. The soil becomes worn out, organic matter is lost, and the soil becomes compacted to such an extent that it cannot adequately support a healthy, vigorous plant. Rose production will decline eventually, in spite of the consistent use of sound horticultural practices.

One method of retarding this gradual deterioration is to periodically rebuild the beds when the roses are dormant. Do this as soon as possible after the spring thaw. This may occur in late April or early May depending on the weather. The bushes should be carefully dug up and

"heeled in" immediately in a sheltered spot. Keep them damp during the renovation period.

Renovation consists of adding organic matter, coarse sand, vermiculite, or perlite, and phosphate fertilizer. Then the rose bed is dug and turned over. Organic matter may be peat moss, well-rotted manure, or compost. The proportions of these will vary from garden to garden depending on the type of soil you have. You need to create a fairly loose loamy soil that will take in water readily, but not pack easily. Be certain to add the soil amendments and the phosphate fertilizer on the soil before the initial digging. The fertilizer can then be worked down into the root zone. Phosphorous fertilizer does not readily leach downward to the roots when applied to the surface. Now, water the bed well. This allows the bed to firm up sufficiently before the bushes are replanted. The total renovation should be completed within a week to ten days.

### GROWING ROSES IN CONTAINERS

Whether you have an outdoor garden or not, you can still grow roses. Almost any kind of rose can be grown in a container. Cultivars that are low and bushy are most suitable, but you can try any rose of your choice. Table 1, ROSES SUITABLE FOR CONTAINER GROWING lists some reliable cultivars that have been grown with success.

Containers for growing the larger roses should be at least 45 - 60 cm (18 - 24 in.)

wide and 40 - 60 cm (16 - 24 in.) deep. For miniatures, 15 - 20 cm (6 - 8 in.) diameter pots are suitable. Wood, clay, or plastic containers are satisfactory. In a pot 60 cm (24 in.) wide and 60 cm (24 in.) deep, you can plant either a Hybrid Tea, 3 Floribundas or up to 12 miniatures (see Figure 15, CONTAINER GARDENING).

A mix of 1 part peat moss, 1 part coarse sand and 2 parts good garden soil is a suitable soil mixture for roses in containers. For good drainage, place a 2.5 cm (1 in.) layer of gravel in the bottom of the container before planting the roses. Make sure there are adequate drainage holes at the bottom of the container.

A rose is planted in a container in the conventional manner with the graft union just below the surface. Outdoor maintenance instructions given elsewhere in this publication do not apply to container grown roses.

Water is required more frequently than for garden grown roses because of the smaller moisture holding reservoir in a pot. For fertilizing suggestions refer to the section on FERTILIZING.

Just before fall freeze-up, move the containerized roses into a root house. If a root house is not available, bury them, pot and all, in a 75 cm (2.5 ft.) deep hole in a well drained location where there is likely to be a good snow cover. The soil must be moist. In spring when the soil has thawed sufficiently, the roses can

## Figure 16
## GROWING UNDER ARTIFICIAL LIGHTS

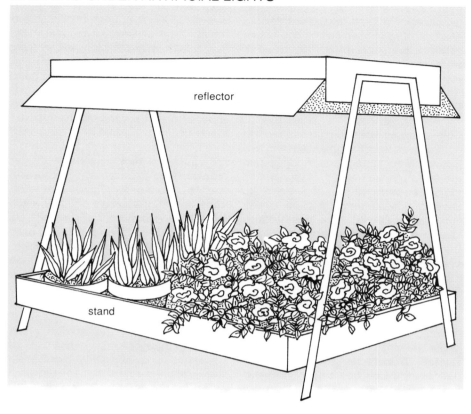

## Figure 17
## PROTECTING NEWLY PLANTED ROSES

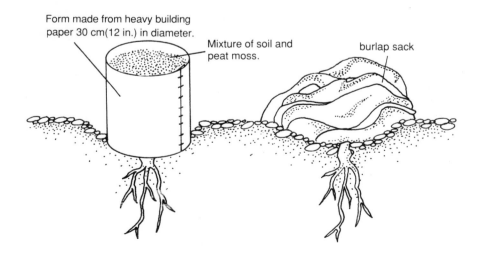

Form made from heavy building paper 30 cm(12 in.) in diameter.

Mixture of soil and peat moss.

burlap sack

be dug up, pruned, and routine maintenance begun.

Roses that have been grown in the same container for 3 - 4 years require re-potting. Re-potting is best done in the spring.

## GROWING UNDER ARTIFICIAL LIGHTS

Miniature roses can be easily grown under fluorescent plant-light bulbs such as Gro-Lux, Vigor Light, Gro-Light, Vita-Lite, Agro-Lite and others. A 1:1 mix of standard fluorescent cool white and fluorescent plant-lights will usually give good growth. This is less expensive than using plant-lights only. Incandescent plant-light bulbs can also be used, but they create a lot of heat, are expensive to operate, and do not last as long as fluorescent bulbs. Regular household incandescent bulbs are not recommended because they are rich in the red and far-red light necessary for flowering, but weak in the blue and violet rays necessary for vegetative growth.

Miniatures are particularly suited to indoor growing because they are small, flower continually, have many colors, are fragrant, and are compatible with other house plants (see Figure 16, GROWING UNDER ARTIFICIAL LIGHTS).

A temperature of 16 - 22°C (60 - 70°F) is suitable for vegetative growth. Temperatures of 2 - 3°C (8 - 10°F) lower encourage flower production. Humidity should be between 50 - 60 percent for optimum growth.

Lighting assemblies can be purchased or fabricated. They should have reflectors of polished aluminum or white enamel. Set the lamps 10 cm (4 in.) apart and 20 cm (8 in.) above the foliage. The lights should be turned on for 12 - 18 hours per day. An 18 hour light period will force faster growth, but 14 hours is a good average.

Pot sizes should be 7.5 cm (3 in.) for the miniature roses and up to 15 cm (6 in.) for larger varieties. A soil mix of 2 parts soil, 3 parts vermiculite, and 1 part peat moss is considered suitable.

## PROTECTING NEWLY PLANTED ROSES

Newly planted rose bushes must be protected against dehydration. It takes two or three weeks after planting under good growing conditions for new roots to form. This is a critical time for the weakened plant. A common way of protecting rose plants is to make cylinders out of heavy building paper about 30 cm (12 in.) tall and 30 cm (12 in.) in diameter (see Figure 17, PROTECTING NEWLY PLANTED ROSES). Fasten the paper together with a stapling gun. Place the cylinder over the plant and fill with a mixture of soil and peat moss. Keep it moist but do not overwater. Leave the paper collar in place until new growth appears. Remove the cylinder and gradually lower the mound of soil giving the new growth time to harden off.

Another simple method of protecting rose plants is to cover them with a burlap sack. It can be readily removed when weather conditions are appropriate. It also eliminates the chore of obtaining, storing, and disposing of a protective soil covering.

If you protect your rose bushes immediately after planting, you will be rewarded with a bumper crop of beautiful blooms.

# MAINTENANCE

Once your roses are planted and growing there are a few routine chores to complete that will enhance their productivity throughout the growing season. You will find the most important of these chores outlined in the following section.

## LATE SPRING FROST PROTECTION

When a late spring frost is predicted, sprouted roses must be protected with some type of cover. Burlap or newspapers provide good protection, but they must be anchored down to prevent winds from blowing them away. Another method is to set out a sprinkler to cover

the desired area. Start the sprinkler just as the temperature reaches the freezing point and leave it on until the temperature returns to above freezing. The critical point often comes one or two hours before sunrise. Overall coverage of the rose bed is necessary for this method to be effective.

## CULTIVATION

Cultivation is routinely necessary to control weeds, prevent diseases, and loosen up the surface soil. Roughing up the soil surface makes it more open to moisture penetration, and helps to develop a more friable medium. Deep cultivation is not recommended because shallow rose roots may be injured.

## WATERING

Rose bushes grow best when they receive an average of 2.5 cm (1 in.) of moisture per week during the hot dry periods of the Prairie growing season. There are times when there is very little rainfall. Supplementary watering is necessary during these periods. A rain gauge is absolutely necessary to determine how much supplementary water is actually required to make up any shortage. A 25 L (5 gal.) pail per plant is equivalent to 2.5 cm (1 in.) of rain.

Roses respond amazingly to adequate feeding and watering. You can avoid periods of reduced flower production if you water and fertilize well.

There are several methods of watering roses. One method is to use an overhead sprinkler. However, this wets the foliage, and wet foliage encourages the spread of diseases such as blackspot, rust, and mildew. Also, sprinkling the entire bed can be a waste of water and ineffective in getting water directly to the roots, unless you have a perfectly level rose bed. A soaker hose can be used but it takes a long time, and, depending on the equipment, it can be difficult to determine how much water has been applied.

The following method is reasonably fast and effective, and the approach personally recommended by the author. After the rose bushes are uncovered in

the spring, contour the soil around each plant and form a saucer, 5 cm (2 in.) deep and 30 - 38 cm (12 - 15 in.) in diameter. Be careful not to expose the roots. A bit of sawdust or peat moss mulch in this depression will prevent rapid evaporation and retain moisture. The saucer-like depression at the base of each bush facilitates easier watering, and it brings the graft union nearer the surface, making it easier for new shoots to emerge.

A 1.2 m (4 ft.) watering wand with a water breaker head provides easy access to bushes up to 2 m (6 ft.) away. Travel up and down the rows filling each saucer-like depression with water. By the time you reach the end, the first ones are ready to receive another filling. Filling each "saucer" four to five times provides close to 23 L (5 gal.) of water. With this method, every plant gets plenty of water where it is needed—throughout the root system.

## FERTILIZING

Newly planted roses are not fertilized until new growth is 5.0 - 7.5 cm (2 - 3 in.) long.

Roses are heavy feeders and their performance, to a great extent, depends on soil fertility and the moisture supply. About May 1 start the season with an ample helping of well-rotted cow manure or other organic matter. Then, begin regular light feedings with a balanced, readily soluble fertilizer with trace elements. Nutrients do not become available to the roots unless they are in solution. Therefore, plenty of water makes the whole process work.

For regular feedings, use a water soluble rose fertilizer such as 20-24-14 or 28-14-14. It is also advisable to add liquid fish fertilizer to the other fertilizer mix. Follow the recommendations on the containers according to the following schedules:
- May 15
- June 30
- July 31

The last fertilization of the year, about mid-August, should help mature and harden off the plants before the cold

## ROSE FERTILIZING - ANOTHER APPROACH
*by G. W. Shewchuk*

*In 1980, to experiment, I fed my roses twice as often at half the rate. It seemed to make sense and the roses appeared to appreciate it, but it does take more time. I used the recommended fertilizer solution at one half the rate according to the following time schedule:*

- *May 15*
- *June 15*
- *June 30*
- *July 15*
- *July 31*

*I gave the larger, older bushes an extra litre or so of the fertilizer solution each time they were fertilized. This is the schedule that I currently use.*

weather sets in. Fertilizers such as 10-30-20 can be used. If this is not available, 10-52-10 is a good substitute. If you have the agricultural formulations of 11-48-0 and 0-0-60 on hand, prepare your own by mixing two parts of 11-48-0 and one part of 0-0-60. Any of these preparations may be used at the rate of one tablespoon in 4.5 L (1 gal.) of water for each rose bush.

One alternative to dissolving commercial fertilizers in water is to apply them dry and water them in. This method does not distribute it as evenly and effectively as fertilizer applied in solution.

Once a year, preferably in the spring, add one tablespoon of micronized iron per 4.5 L (1 gal.) of fertilizer mix. This is insurance against rose bushes becoming anemic or chlorotic. Iron deficiency is quite common in roses, especially when grown in soil with a pH of 7.5 or higher, and an excess of lime or phosphorus. This condition is aggravated by excessive use of unbalanced fertilizers and high calcium water. A high calcium content is common in many Prairie well water and city supply systems. Iron deficiency symptoms are:

- Yellowing of new foliage that later turns cream colored.
- Mature leaves that are yellow with dark green veins.

Some rose enthusiasts use "cow tea" to fertilize their roses. "Cow tea" is made in a 205 L (45 gal.) barrel. Place 11 kg (25 lb.) of cow manure in the barrel and fill with water, stirring occasionally. In a week the "cow tea" is ready to use. Keep the barrel covered so the neighbors cannot take offence at the stench. After about three fillings, the barrel will need to be recharged with fresh manure. Be careful not to overdo a good thing. Before full strength "cow tea" is used, dilute it with water until it has the appearance of weak tea.

There is a good substitute for this: two cups of alfalfa meal per plant per year. "Alfalfa tea" is also a good, odorless substitute for cow tea. Make it by soaking 4 cups alfalfa pellets in 25 L (5 gal.) of water for three days. Give each rose bush 4.5 L (1 gal.) of alfalfa tea first thing in the spring and again a month later. The alfalfa leaves that are left at the bottom of your container are still good for another mix. Add another 25 L (5 gal.) of water and in three days you have more alfalfa tea. It sounds like a pretty good idea and the roses seem to benefit from it. You will not have to put up with a big barrel and the stench.

There are a few proponents of foliar feeding, and each year somebody says that he has found the answer to quick and cheap fertilization. Cheap, because very small amounts of nutrients are used in the water spray. This method cannot provide all the requirements, however, because roses are heavy feeders. Foliar feeding can only effectively supply the micronutrients such as iron, manganese, and magnesium, which are required in very small quantities.

## MICRONUTRIENT DEFICIENCY

Chlorosis (yellowing of leaves) may be caused by a lack of iron or manganese in the soil. This can be the result of years of cropping without replacing these essential elements or growing roses in alkaline soil. Iron and manganese supplements can be obtained from garden supply shops. It should be borne in mind that deficiency of nitrogen can also cause yellowing of the leaves. Check the nitrogen level and the pH (alkalinity or acidity) of the soil.

For soils deficient in magnesium, or in rose beds older than three years, annually add one half tablespoon of Epsom Salt (magnesium sulfate) per plant in a water solution, in addition to the regular feeding. Heavy rains and the use of alkaline city water seem to deplete the availability of magnesium so essential for growth.

## MULCHING

If your garden has good soil that retains adequate moisture, plus good drainage, aeration, and a humus balance, it really does not need a mulch. If this is not the case, however, a good mulch will add many more roses to your rose bed.

Mulching can provide the following benefits:

- Permit water and air to pass through easily
- Reduce compaction
- Add humus
- Provide good soil insulation
- Keep the soil and roots cool
- Maintain a high level of moisture
- Prevent soil splattering onto the rose bushes during a rain or watering.

In Canada, shredded peat moss provides all these benefits adequately. There are also other mulches that can be used:

- sawdust
- wood chips
- leaves
- chopped straw and hay
- tree bark
- manure.

Mulches should be applied to rose beds to a depth of 2.5 - 5.0 cm (1 - 2 in.) (see Figure 18, MULCHING ROSES).

Mulch is not a substitute for the water required by roses, but it does reduce the moisture loss. A good mulch reduces the number of waterings required. A mulch also serves as an insulator from the intense heat of the sun and helps to maintain a cool and more even soil temperature.

The author uses peat moss as a winter cover, but it is difficult to pick it all up in the spring. Since it makes a good mulch,

## Figure 18
## MULCHING ROSES

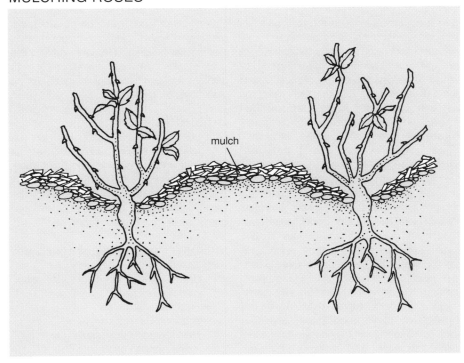

mulch

it is practical to leave some of it on after spring clean-up. If you have access to cheap or free sawdust, do the same with it. Peat moss and sawdust also look quite presentable in the rose beds and do not produce an unsightly mess if used.

### BASIC PRUNING

In our cold and extreme weather, very few, if any, tender rose canes survive above the protective winter cover. A protective winter cover is recommended under the OVERWINTERING ROSES section. In this case the need for pruning is not urgent. However, there are hardy shrub roses that send out numerous new canes each year and require annual regenerative pruning.

Shrub rose canes become less productive with age, somewhat like gooseberry and currant bushes. Therefore, it is desirable to encourage the development of new canes. To do this, remove one old cane each year and permit a new one to replace it (see Figure 19, PRUNING ROSES). This will eventually produce a shrub with a range of canes from 1 - 5 years old.

### GENERAL GUIDELINES

Keep these guidelines in mind when pruning (see Figure 19, PRUNING ROSES):

- Use a good, sharp, scissor-type pruner to get a clean cut. The anvil-type tends to crush the ends of the stems. Dull pruners will mash the stems and such wounds will not heal well and are subject to infection and die-back.
- Remove damaged, diseased, or dead wood. Cut back to sound wood that shows white or greenish pith.
- Direct the growth of the canes by making the cut 6.0 mm (0.25 in.) above an eye or leaf bud located in the direction you want the new branch to grow.
- Prune so that the center of the bush is open to the sun and air.
- Remove crossing, twiggy or frail side growth.
- Leave 5 - 10 healthy canes distributed evenly at the base.
- Look at and study each bush carefully before cutting; once the cane is cut it cannot be replaced.
- Local climatic conditions dictate

the best pruning time. On the Prairies this period usually extends from April 20 to early May depending on location and weather conditions.
- Often two or three buds emerge from the same point on a rose cane. Leaving multiple shoots such as this results in double or triple headed canes. Generally, all are weak and subject to splitting under heavy rain or wind stress. It is a good practice to remove all but the largest shoots before they get too big. This can be done by rubbing out those not required.

If you examine a rose cane closely, you will find that every central bud has two side bud marks. Nature has provided these potential buds to guard against the loss of a primary bud. As a rule these potential buds remain dormant as long as the primary bud is active. Under normal conditions these potential buds do not develop.

### REMOVING OLD BLOOMS

For stronger and healthier rose bushes that produce larger quantities of blossoms, old spent flowers should be removed. This is particularly important right after the first flush of spring bloom is gone. Removing the spent flowers quickly helps plants produce new canes immediately.

The removal of dead blooms should be carried out with the same care and attention as basic pruning. Cut to a bud, which means just 6.0 mm (0.25 in.) above a leaf that shelters a live bud. Never make a cut half way between the leaves. Cut dead blooms to the first leaf with a good bud as shown in Figure 19, PRUNING ROSES. Cut flowers from new bushes with short stems usually back to the first or second leaf. Established roses can be cut back even up to the second leaf from the base if desired. Cut only a few stems this low; leave the rest fairly long. **It takes at least seven leaves to manufacture enough food to produce each flower.** That is why leaves should not be removed unnecessarily. The plant needs its leaves. There is an old saying among rose growers that goes like this: "She

Figure 19
PRUNING ROSES

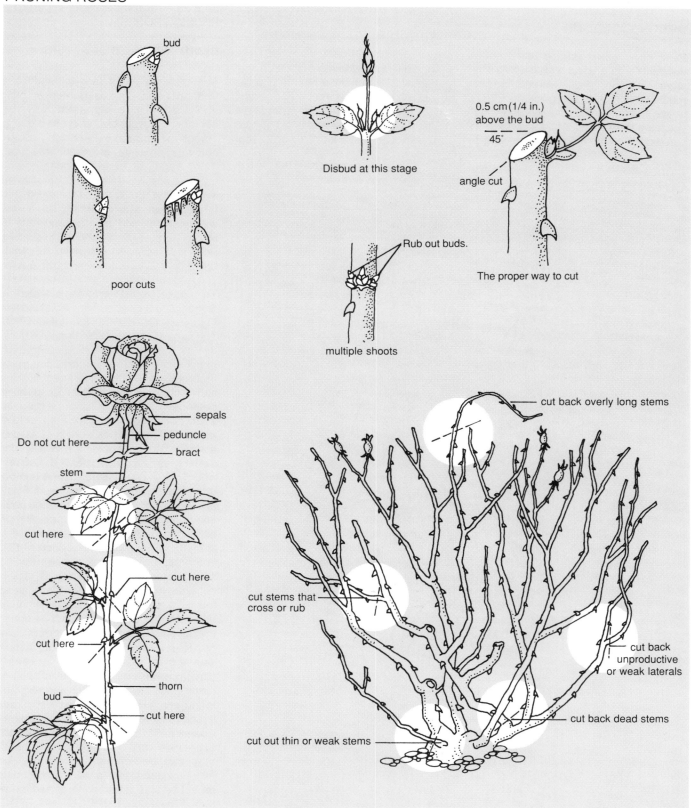

bud

poor cuts

Disbud at this stage

0.5 cm (1/4 in.)
above the bud
45°

angle cut

The proper way to cut

Rub out buds.

multiple shoots

sepals

peduncle

Do not cut here

bract

stem

cut here

cut here

cut here

thorn

bud

cut here

cut back overly long stems

cut stems that
cross or rub

cut back
unproductive
or weak laterals

cut back dead stems

cut out thin or weak stems

loved them to death, cutting every long stem that appeared."

## CUTTING BLOOMS

Very often you have to make tough decisions—do you cut a rose with a long stem and ignore the plant's growth requirements, or do you place the plant's needs first? This is your decision. Do you want to sacrifice future growth or do you want to maintain a healthy plant to produce numerous blooms for several years? Figure 20, CUTTING ROSE BLOOMS, illustrates judicious cutting.

## DISBUDDING

Disbudding is a pruning technique that perfectionists and show people practice to obtain a single, large, near-perfect bloom on Hybrid Teas and Grandiflora roses. If you allow the whole set of buds to bloom, you get a lot of color in your garden. Disbudding is done three weeks before a show so that the scars heal prior to presentation (see Figure 19, PRUNING ROSES).

## BLIND WOOD, BLIND TIPS

Sometimes a shoot fails to produce a terminal bud. This is termed a "blind end". Where no apparent physical damage is noticeable, it is often due to insect or disease damage. Some cultivars produce more "blind ends", "blind wood", or "blind tips" than others (see Figure 21, NORMAL VS. BLIND TIP). Some do it in early spring and others soon after planting. In a few weeks, blind end plants may start to bloom normally, with shoots originating from side sprouts below the terminal "blind tip".

To induce normal growth, cut back a "blind tip" to a good bud immediately (see Figure 22, CORRECTING BLIND TIPS). The sooner it is done, the better.

In the rose literature, you may find many theories about "blind wood" but no satisfactory explanation. The author's personal explanation is presented for your consideration. In the 1930's, farmers on the Prairies were plagued with a similar phenomenon. A normally high yielding variety of oats called "Victory" would occasionally have a large number of aborted florets, called "blossom blast" in those days. This reduced the potentially high yield expected. It was explained by field crop specialists that something happened to reduce critical nutrients. This may have been due to cold, heat, drought, or an actual lack of nutrients in the soil. Rather than having the collapse of the whole plant, nature has provided a partial abandonment of the development of its fruit (flowers). As previously mentioned, in Victory oats it was termed "blossom blast"; in roses it can be called "blind wood", "blind tips", or "blind ends". Until definite answers are found for "blind wood", keep the rose bushes well fed, and diseases and pests under control. Should "blind wood" appear on very small and short canes, they can be ignored or cut off. On heavier canes, the "blind wood" should be cut back to a leaf-node or two below (see Figure 22, CORRECTING BLIND

## Figure 20
## CUTTING ROSE BLOOMS

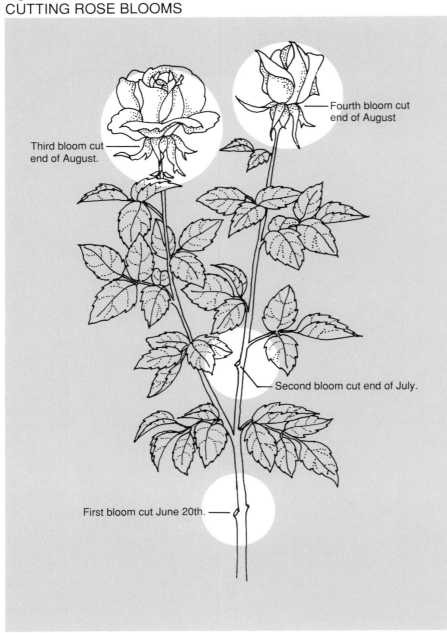

Third bloom cut end of August.

Fourth bloom cut end of August

Second bloom cut end of July.

First bloom cut June 20th.

Figure 21
NORMAL VS. BLIND TIP

Figure 22
CORRECTING BLIND TIPS

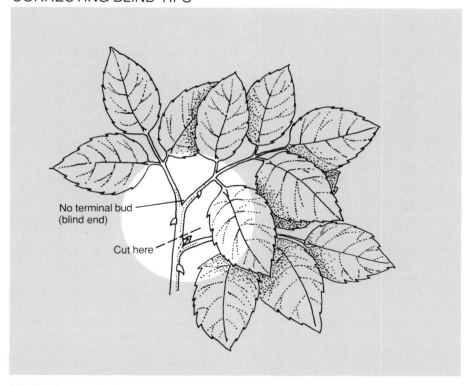

No terminal bud
(blind end)

Cut here

## HOW TO KEEP ROSE BUSHES BLOOMING

The basic step for long blooming roses is to use cultivars noted for their florescence and continuity of bloom. The Floribundas such as Iceberg, Frensham, Fire King, and Europeana, and the Polyantha, The Fairy, are noted for this feature. As a rule, Hybrid Tea roses are less florescent than the Floribundas. Even among the Hybrid Teas there are cultivars which have a greater tendency for repeat blooming than the others. The common popular old cultivars fall into this category. The fact that they have remained popular for so many years is proof enough that they possess this desirable habit.

To ensure a plentiful number of blooms from spring until freeze-up, there are a number of procedures to follow. Follow these steps to keep roses blooming profusely:
  • Plant properly and protect the rose bushes as previously recommended.
  • Feed according to the recommended schedule.
  • Water regularly, making certain that the roses receive at least 2.5 cm (1 in.) per week.
  • Control pests.
  • Remove old spent flowers quickly.
  • Use continuous blooming cultivars.
  • Winterize your roses, for annual repeat performance.

## SUCKERS

At times canes with different foliage emerge from the root stock on which the rose is grown. These are called suckers. Suckers have small pale leaves bearing seven or more serrated leaflets, originating from below the graft union. A sucker that is not removed may quickly overtake the upper portion of the plant and completely dominate it. Suckers tend to be tall, vigorous, and unproductive of blossoms.

Quite often a sucker can be pulled up completely without doing much damage to the root system. If pulling is not successful, dig a small hole at the base of the plant. Cut the sucker off flush with the root, as shown in Figure 23,

TIPS). The cutting back to a leaf-node stimulates the development of a new bud. If done early enough in the season, the new cane becomes a productive one. If left alone, the "blind tip" remains until fall. The best that can be expected is for the rose to produce a side shoot at a very late date. Quite often it is too late for the production of a bloom.

Figure 23
SUCKERS

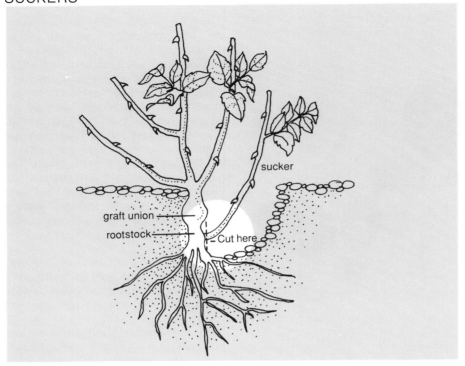

Figure 24
STAKING ROSES

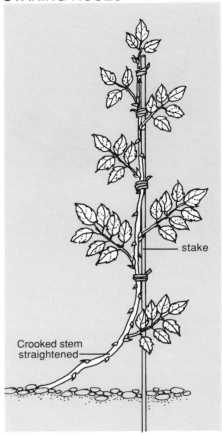

SUCKERS. If any of it is left, it will continue growing.

## STAKING AND LABELLING

Tall rose canes growing in unprotected areas may require support to avoid wind damage. Do this by inserting a narrow 1 m (3 ft.) stake into the ground near the center of the bush. Tie the more vulnerable canes to the stake using "Twist-ties". Where the roses have good protection, only the tallest canes may benefit from staking. Young willows make beautiful stakes. Treat the lower 15 cm (6 in.) of the stakes with a wood preservative so they last for several years.

For show purposes, rose stems must be straight. Crooked stems can be straightened by tying the stem to a stake in at least three different places (see Figure 24, STAKING ROSES). This should be done about two weeks before the show. "Twist-ties" are handy for this purpose.

After growing roses for a few years, you will realize that each cultivar has some distinguishing features. Make a point of identifying any cultivar that has impressed you. When Chrysler Imperial is mentioned you will come to associate that name with a beautifully shaped dark red fragrant rose; Peace—a large, showy attractive blend of yellow, pink, and white. Label your roses to help establish this habit. Knowing the name of a rose you saw at a flower show or in some garden makes it much easier to find in nursery catalogues and nurseries.

A purchased rose often has a tag bearing its name wired to one of the canes. After planting, this tag should be removed and fastened to a stake nearby. Never leave it on the cane because the wire tie can choke the cane when it starts to grow. Inconspicuous, green or brown stakes and labels are advisable with the rose variety printed on them with a water-proof marker. Naming can also be done with key numbers that refer to a printed list.

# OVERWINTERING ROSES

## WINTERING TENDER ROSES

Winter protection is absolutely necessary for tender roses on the Prairies. Resistance to winter kill is dependent upon the variety, the hardiest being the wild and shrub roses. Among the garden cultivars, the Floribundas generally survive somewhat better than the others when unprotected.

The following method has proven successful for wintering Hybrid Teas, Grandifloras, Floribundas, and Polyanthas.

Tender Hybrid Teas, Grandifloras, and Floribundas do not really fully prepare for winter as our native plants do. They grow and bloom continually until severe cold brings them to a halt. This makes them vulnerable to winter kill. Stop the use of fertilizer in late August, and restrict water after mid-September to help them harden off for the winter.

If the soil is dry in **late fall** (approximately, October 20), give the rose bushes a good soaking just before

## Figure 25
## ROSES COVERED WITH PEAT MOSS

winter sets in and the soil freezes. In fact, give all perennials a good soaking at this time. Most years the soil freezes around the end of October or early November. The rose tops should then be cut down to a height of 25 - 30 cm (10 - 12 in.). The cuttings should be destroyed. This pruning contributes considerably to the prevention and carry-over of diseases and insects that may be present.

The bud graft union requires the most protection. Cover the graft union and the lower canes with insulating material to a minimum depth of 25 - 35 cm (10 - 12 in.) (see Figure 25, ROSES COVERED WITH PEAT MOSS). The aim of mounding or covering is not to protect them from freezing, but to protect them from premature thawing, and repeated freezing and thawing. They may be hilled like potatoes, if they are spaced far enough apart and the rose roots are not exposed by doing this. If they are planted close together, you will have to get soil from some other place. A vegetable garden nearby would be very handy. However, I find that peat moss is much easier to apply and remove than soil. Sawdust could be substituted for peat moss. In addition, peat moss and sawdust do not appear to freeze and thaw as readily as soil. A 100 L (4 cu. ft.) sack of peat moss will cover 8 to 10 rose

bushes. If wind is a problem, cover the hills with a bit of hay, straw, spruce boughs, or better still, burlap/gunny sack material (see Figure 26, ROSES COVERED WITH PEAT MOSS AND BURLAP). In places where neatness and tidiness is of no major concern, use straw or hay over the peat moss to a depth of 25 - 30 cm (10 - 12 in.) (see Figure 27, STRAW COVERING). Dust

powdered sulfur over each plant to discourage mice.

A good snow cover adds considerable protection. On roses where the snow cover is thin, you can spread sidewalk, driveway, or drifted snow over them. Do not use snow that has had a chemical de-icer applied to it.

During mild spells you may have difficulty keeping an adequate snow cover on rose beds in front of south facing buildings or other structures. It is not the cold that kills rose bushes, but the repeated freezing and thawing that occurs in early spring. The covering recommended above should keep the soil frozen until the final spring thaw.

Planting with the graft union 10 cm (4 in.) below ground level permits the use of minimum coverage and at the same time provides sufficient winter protection. Using the recommended method, the author lost only 7 out of 300 in the spring of 1979, and 5 out of 315 in 1980. Most of those lost were eight years old or older. It is not known how long tender roses are likely to live on the Prairies. These may have died of old age. The author has some rose bushes up to 14 years old that were planted and protected as recommended.

## Figure 26
## ROSES COVERED WITH PEAT MOSS AND BURLAP

## Figure 27
## STRAW COVERING

### OVERCOMING PLANTING PROBLEMS

The advice and instructions for planting on packaged roses are usually meant for rose growers in areas where winters are very mild.

If roses have been planted with the graft union above the ground level as recommended in most books, or as shown on containers of packaged roses, one of the following methods will have to be used to get them through the winter safely:

### Method 1:
After the frost has killed the foliage, cut the canes down to 30 cm (1 ft.) in height. Label the plants with a water-proof marker. Dig them up and bury them in the garden or some other convenient spot at a depth of 1 m (2 - 3 ft.). Be certain that you do not bury them where water is likely to pool after a spring thaw. In spring when the tree buds are about to burst into leaf, dig them up and replant. Digging the roses in this manner destroys a lot of the fine roots and sets them back significantly.

### Method 2:
After the frost has killed the foliage, cover the plant with insulating material such as hay, peat moss, sawdust, or wheat straw to a depth of 60 cm (2 ft.).

In spring when the native trees are about to burst into leaf, uncover, prune, and clean up.

### REMOVAL OF WINTER PROTECTIVE COVER

This is an important spring chore often overlooked, especially where soil is used as a covering for winter protection. Remove covering some time between

## Figure 28
## BURLAP REMOVED IN SPRING

April 12 and April 20 **depending on how early the native tree buds are starting to burst out into leaf** (see Figure 28, BURLAP REMOVED IN SPRING). You will probably be able to recover about 80 percent of your original covering provided you have not lost any due to wind erosion (see Figure 29, PEAT MOSS REMOVED).

Around each rose bush, hollow out a shallow depression 30 - 45 cm (12 - 18 in.) in diameter and 4 - 5 cm (1.5 - 2 in.) deep to facilitate:
• Watering
• Fertilizing
• The emergence of new shoots from below ground.

Many good roses are weakened and actually lost because of the failure to remove soil covering the bush.

Occasionally there may be a threatening frost after the roses are uncovered. Should this happen, be prepared to cover your bushes with burlap, paper, or canvas tarp. Burlap is perhaps best because it is a good insulator and is easy to handle, store, and re-use.

### WINTERING POTTED ROSES

Potted roses may be wintered successfully by using one of two methods:

Figure 29
PEAT MOSS REMOVED

Figure 30
SPADES AND TROWELS

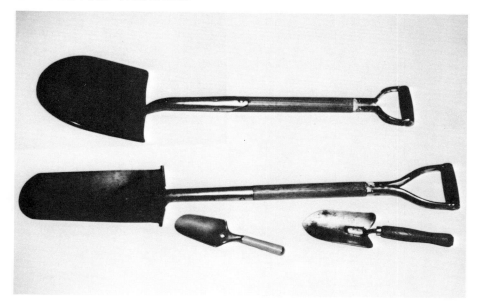

## WINTERING STANDARD TREE ROSES

Standard or Tree roses are considerably more difficult to winter than Hybrid Teas or Floribundas. Their graft union is on a stem standard 1 - 1.2 m (3 - 4 ft.) above the root system. To successfully overwinter standard roses the graft union must be protected with at least 30 cm (1 ft.) of soil or some other insulating material.

To provide this protection, you must follow one of two methods.

**Method 1:**
Plant in a normal way. In the fall, when frost threatens to kill all growth, dig them out with as much of the root system as possible. Bury them horizontally with moist soil in a pit at least 60 cm (2 ft.) deep. In early spring dig them up and replant.

**Method 2:**
Plant the roses in containers, 25 L (5 gal.) size or larger. In the fall, at about freeze-up time, either bury them horizontally or store in a root house as suggested previously for other potted roses.

## TOOLS FOR THE ROSE GARDENER

Gardening tools should be viewed as a long-lasting investment. The best advice is to buy good tools. When not in use, keep them clean and under cover so that the wooden handles do not deteriorate and the metal does not rust. At the end of the season rub all metal parts with an oiled cloth and wooden handles with linseed oil.

### SPADE

A spade for the garden is like a plow for the farm. It is a heavy duty tool used in the preparation of rose beds and for digging planting holes. A narrow-nosed spade is used for digging in confined areas. Sharpen a spade regularly for easier digging.

**Method 1:**
Dig a 60 cm (2 ft.) deep trench. The plant and pot are laid down horizontally then completely covered with moist soil. In early spring, they are dug up and standard maintenance procedures started again. Potted roses can also be wintered following the procedures suggested for other hybrids.

**Method 2:**
If you are fortunate enough to have access to a root house, you have an ideal place to overwinter potted roses. Just prior to complete freeze-up, store the rose, pot and all, in the root house. In the spring, replace up to 7.5 cm (3 in.) of the surface soil, water the plant, and it is off to another good start.

## Figure 31
## SUPER WEEDER

### RAKE

A rake is mainly used for cleaning up loose debris, breaking up soil lumps and levelling rose beds in preparation for planting.

### HAND TROWEL

This is a useful tool for soil mixing and filling in the holes when planting roses (see Figure 30, SPADES AND TROWELS).

### HOE

The purpose of the common garden hoe is for cultivating and keeping weeds down. You may have used a standard hoe and found that, within a day or two, many weeds were recovering from the hoeing. Actually they may have been covered with soil and/or transplanted. If you have had this problem, you'll appreciate the SUPER WEEDER illustrated in Figure 31, SUPER WEEDER. Not only will it cut weeds pushing and pulling, but it also leaves the weeds loose on the surface. The problem is that you cannot buy one. (The writer turned down an offer of $125.00 for the one shown in this book.) However, plans for making this type and a smaller model giving all essential measurements and specifications may be obtained from

the University of Alberta, Faculty of Extension (see RESOURCE MATERIALS for details).

Hundreds of gardeners have made this hoe or have had a friend make one for them and have never regretted it. Hoeing **almost** becomes a pleasure using this SUPER WEEDER. Try it on seedling weeds, on tough tall ones and on some grass sod. You will have to admit that

## Figure 32
## PRUNING TOOLS

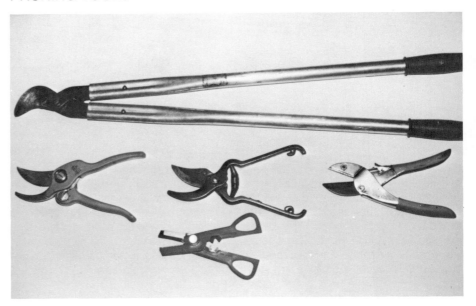

it's the neatest, easiest, fastest hoe you've ever used.

### WHEELBARROW

When you start working in the garden, the need for moving all sorts of things arises; moving away discarded soil and sub-soil and bringing in your soil mix are examples. You can prepare a soil mix in the wheelbarrow if you wish. If you do not like the one-wheeler, which tips easily, there is a very handy, very manouverable two-wheel cart available.

### GLOVES

You will soon discover that gloves are absolutely necessary when working with roses. Those with leather palms and heavy duty cotton backs serve the purpose well. Good leather gloves are better but much more expensive.

### PRUNERS

There are many types of pruners on the market. The best for the rose gardener are the scissor-action type. When sharp, they make a clean cut. The anvil type have the tendency to crush the rose cane, especially if they are not sharp. The long-handled pruners (loppers) are used for heavy canes and difficult work where it is not convenient to use a saw (see Figure 32, PRUNING TOOLS).

## DUSTER

Dusters come in a great variety of types and sizes (see Figure 33, SPRAYER, DUSTER, AND PESTICIDES). As with sprayers, get one to match your garden: a small one for a few plants and a larger one for a bigger garden. The one shown here is suitable for small and average home gardens. Another thing that is unique about this duster is that it can also be used as a small sprayer. It does not corrode, rust, or clog. It is easy to load or empty just by removing the end cap.

## SPRAYER

Sprayers are available in many sizes and types, ranging from the half-litre index finger, trigger operated, up to four-litre, ten-litre, and larger sized hand pump type sprayers. The half-litre may be adequate for anyone with no more than half a dozen rose bushes. The four-litre size may be good for up to 20 to 25 bushes and the ten-litre size for 50 or more rose bushes. When buying a sprayer, choose one made of plastic or stainless steel. Clean them out after every use and they'll be trouble-free and last a long time. The sprayer in Figure 33, SPRAYER, DUSTER, AND PESTICIDES, is stainless steel. It has been used for 18 years and looks good enough to last another 18 years.

## WATER HOSE

Anyone with more than six rose bushes needs a water hose. The length required depends on how far the roses are from the water source. Whatever the length, get a cord-reinforced rubber hose. You will pay a little more for this than for a plastic one, but you'll have no problems with stiff, hard-to-handle plastic. You will also find that it will outlast several plastic hoses.

## WATER WAND

The wand can be fitted with water breakers for fine, medium and coarse, gentle rain-like watering. It can also be fitted with a nozzle that forces a strong upward spray, useful for the control of spider mites. The wands come in various lengths.

## WATER PAILS and BARRELS

Metal or plastic pails of the 10 - 20 L size (2 - 4 gal.) are very handy for carrying water and preparing fertilizer solutions. Containers or barrels holding 70 - 205 L (15 - 45 gal.) for preparing alfalfa and cow tea are required by anyone growing 100 rose bushes or more.

## NAME STAKES

There are many kinds of name stakes you can buy at garden shops. You can also make stakes. They can be made out of 2.5 cm (1 in.) thick cedar lumber, 30 cm (1 ft.) long. They are cut 6 to 7 mm (1/4 in.) thick on a fine-toothed power circular saw. The stakes come out very smooth and require no sanding. They are sharpened and then dipped in a green wood preservative. The stakes are allowed to dry before use. A water-proof marker, china marker and a thick soft-lead beginner's pencil make good and long-lasting name markings (see Figure 34, NAME STAKES). Cedar stakes last for several years and are inconspicuous in the garden. When the lettering becomes faded, it can be renewed by a light sanding and re-writing.

## PLANT SUPPORT STAKES

Bamboo stakes, 70 to 90 cm (up to 3 ft.) in height, are long-lasting and the best for supporting rose bush canes. However, much more inexpensive stakes can be made from willow saplings found along roadside ditches in wooded areas. When dried, and dipped in a wood preservative, they will last 2 - 3 years.

## TWIST-TIES

Plastic coated Twist-ties in dispensing rolls are handy for every gardener, especially rose growers. They may be cut to any required length. They are ideal for securing weak, long, and heavily-laden canes to stakes. The plastic-coated kind, if saved, can be used for several years (see Figure 34, NAME STAKES).

## ROSE BED COVER

A cover made of porous material is required for the rose bed during the winterization process. After the peat moss has been applied in late fall, the bushes are then covered to prevent the peat moss from being blown away by the wind. For a few rose bushes an old bed sheet will make do. For larger numbers burlap sacking material is the best. It will last up to five years provided that after use it is dried and stored in a dry place.

Figure 33
## SPRAYER, DUSTER, AND PESTICIDES

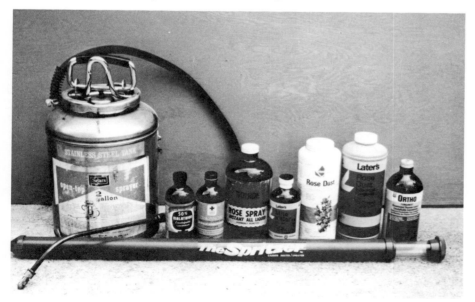

## Figure 34
## NAME STAKES

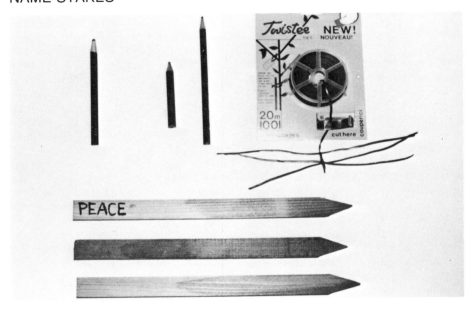

### KNEE PADS

Knee pads provide comfort for gardeners when planting roses or when kneeling and doing other gardening tasks.

### PEAT STORAGE BOX

A box large enough to hold the peat moss or other covering used to protect your rose bushes over winter is required. You may be surprised at how much covering material can be recovered. For 100 roses, the dimension of the box would have to be at least 1 m³ (3 - 4 ft.³). Base the size of the storage box on the number of roses you grow. If you don't have a box, peat moss may be held over from one year to the next, in the original plastic bags if they have not been badly damaged. Once you have winterized your roses, you will have a good idea of what size storage box or boxes are needed. If the peat moss cannot be saved in the spring, you will have to buy more peat moss every year.

### RAIN GAUGE

In order to determine the amount of supplementary water required each week, a rain gauge or other straight sided container is an absolute necessity. Place the gauge in an open unsheltered area.

Radio and TV broadcasts provide only regional or district rainfall averages, and there is often a sizable difference between these figures and the actual rainfall at any given location. Keep your own records and water accordingly.

## PEST CONTROL

The best policy to follow as far as pest control is concerned is one of prevention. This means spraying or dusting to keep both insects and diseases in check from the very beginning. Even though it is generally not recommended to spray before a problem appears, roses are known to be susceptible to insect and disease problems. Therefore, where roses are concerned, preventative sprays are recommended. Spray every week to ten days, covering the tops and undersides of leaves completely. Follow through; do not let pest problems get started.

### INSECTS

Many common garden pests love roses. They include:
- aphids
- caterpillars
- leafcutter bees
- leafhoppers
- minute pirate bugs
- pear slugs
- spider mites (red spiders)
- rose curculio (weevil)
- slugs
- tarnished plant bugs
- thrips.

### APHIDS

Aphids appear throughout the growing season in green or dark brown clusters that take on a black appearance in late August and September. Plants lose vigor and are sometimes stunted; the leaves show yellowing, curling, or puckering; and the flowers and buds become deformed. Aphids secrete a sticky, shiny, honey-dew substance that will be readily noticeable in a sizable infestation.

Aphids are slow moving, soft bodied, winged or wingless, pear-shaped insects up to 6.0 mm (0.25 in.) long. They suck plant juices from the tender terminal shoots and buds, and seek cover underneath the foliage. The honeydew they exude attracts ants and carriers of bacterial, fungal, and viral diseases (see Figure 35, APHID).

### CATERPILLARS

Ordinarily caterpillars feed on the native Trembling Aspen (White Poplar), Willows, and fruit trees. However, because of their voracious appetite they quickly defoliate their original host trees and shrubs, and move to adjacent food sources. They love roses, too, and in

## Figure 35
## APHID

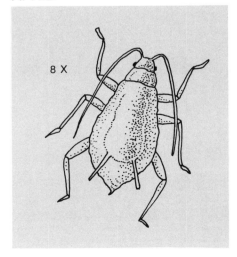

8 X

## Figure 36
## CATERPILLAR

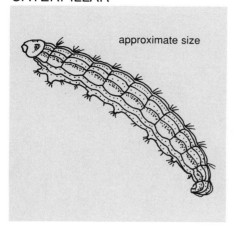

approximate size

their migration can quickly consume the rose foliage and blossoms if left unchecked (see Figure 36, CATERPILLAR).

Caterpillars are the larvae of various butterflies and moths. Perhaps the most damaging are the brown, Tent Caterpillars and the fluffy, black and yellow striped, Woolybear Caterpillars.

Any of the common insecticides effectively control caterpillars. The problem of treatment arises when the caterpillars migrate. In this case, a long-lasting, systemic insecticide such as Cygon or Dimethoate is best and will require applications less frequently. Controlling caterpillars on trees and shrubs in the vicinity will reduce the infestation and problem in the rose garden.

### LEAFCUTTER BEES

The damage done by these insects is easily detectable by the circular shaped notches cut out of the rose leaflets. The insect uses these pieces of rose leaves to line and patch up the wood tunnels they make for rearing their young. These insects are very shy, and they do their leaf-cutting job quickly. The leaf-cutter bee looks like a half sized hornet (see Figure 37, LEAFCUTTER BEE).

### LEAFHOPPERS

Plants infested by leafhoppers look stippled, stunted, lack vigor, and lose color. The leaves become crinkled and

## Figure 37
## LEAFCUTTER BEE

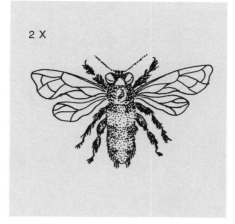

2 X

curled, and may show white dots or blotches. The underside of leaves show dark specks of excrement.

Leafhoppers are 4 - 6 mm (0.16 - 0.25 in.) long, wedge shaped, greenish yellow, whitish, or grey. Some are spotted or banded. They suck from the underside of leaves, and hop away when disturbed. Leafhoppers carry and spread many plant diseases, especially viruses. Several broods are produced each year (see Figure 38, LEAFHOPPER).

## Figure 38
## LEAFHOPPER

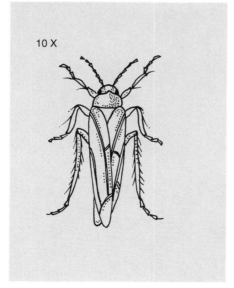

10 X

MINUTE PIRATE BUGS or FLOWER BUGS

These bugs are found on a variety of flowers or under loose bark and in leaf litter. Although they are generally known as predators on other insects and their eggs, they do exercise their piercing mouths on the tender terminal growth and flower buds of roses. They have also been reported to occasionally bite humans. The result is worse than a mosquito sting and more like a black fly bite. Damage done by these insects appears in the form of deformed leaves, spots on leaves, blackened terminal shoots, drooping buds that die, blasted buds, damaged flower bud tops, and imperfect flowers.

These insects are black with white markings, and very small, about 3.0 mm (1/8 in.) long. Their wings fold flat over the abdomen. They have piercing, sucking mouth parts. They go through several phases of metamorphosis; the nymphs (young) resemble the adults except for their smaller size and the absence of wings. The antenna are about 1/4 the length of the body (see Figure 39, MINUTE PIRATE BUG).

PEAR SLUGS

These insects eat the top leaf layer and leave behind a thin transparent

## Figure 39
## MINUTE PIRATE BUG

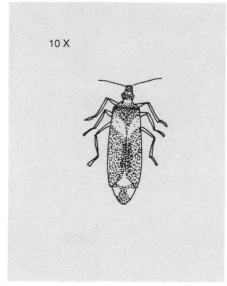

10 X

Figure 40
PEAR SLUG

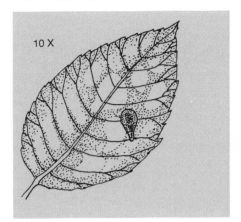

10 X

Figure 41
SPIDER MITE DAMAGE

Figure 42
SPIDER MITE

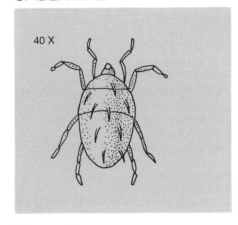

40 X

membrane. Large populations of pear slugs can readily defoliate a rose bush.

Pear slugs look like miniature garden slugs, with the head end thicker than the body. They are dark and slimy, and about 6.0 mm (0.25 in.) long when mature. Usually two generations of pear slugs are produced in a year (see Figure 40, PEAR SLUG).

SPIDER MITES (RED SPIDER)

Silky cobwebs on the underside of leaves, in the leaf axis, and sometimes covering the whole shoot are indications of red spider infestation. When severely infested, leaves show pale spots on the upper side, appear mottled, speckled, or dusty, and will eventually turn yellow or brown and fall off (see Figure 41, SPIDER MITE DAMAGE).

Figure 43
WEEVIL DAMAGE

Figure 44
ROSE CURCULIO

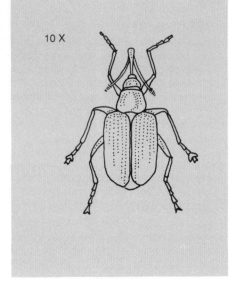

10 X

Figure 45
SLUG

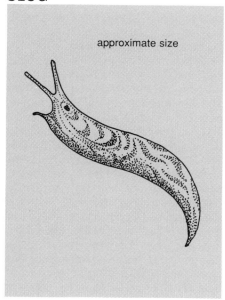

approximate size

Figure 46
TARNISHED PLANT BUG

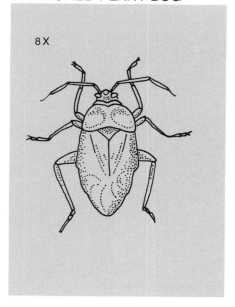

8 X

Figure 47
THRIP

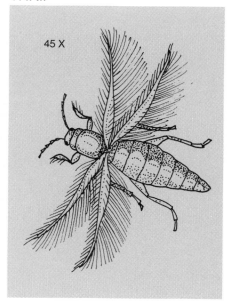

45 X

Spider mites are not really insects. They are related to spiders, ticks, and scorpions, but for convenience most people group them with insects. Spider mites may be brown, green, yellow, red, or black, and are oval shaped and wingless. They are slow moving and less than 1 mm (0.04 in.) in length. They feed by sucking on the underside of the leaves. Spider mites reproduce rapidly, and may produce many generations a year especially when the weather is hot and dry. The hard-to-see spider mites can sometimes be easily detected by tapping leaves over a piece of white paper (see Figure 42, SPIDER MITE).

ROSE CURCULIO (WEEVIL)

When you find rose buds pierced through their sides, you know this beetle is around, whether you see it or not. The bud is probed with the beetle's proboscis in search of rose juice. Perforated buds wilt and dry or fail to open (see Figure 43, WEEVIL DAMAGE).

The insect is a 6.0 mm (0.25 in.) long, reddish brown to black, hard bodied, long nosed beetle. It moves slowly, plays dead, and falls to the ground when disturbed (see Figure 44, ROSE CURCULIO).

SLUGS

In the past few years, slugs have invaded many gardens to such an extent that it is difficult to grow many of the popular plants.

They feed on and damage the foliage of most garden plants. They may be grey, orange, or black, and vary in size from 3 - 10 cm (1 in. - 4 in.). Their movement is very slow and they leave behind silvery, slimy trails. During the day they hide out under debris or litter of some kind in a dark, damp location. They come out of hiding at night or during damp, cloudy weather to feed (see Figure 45, SLUG).

TARNISHED PLANT BUGS

Damage done by these insects is similar to that of Minute Pirate Bugs.

The mature bugs are 6.0 mm (0.25 in.) long, and are flattish and oval shaped. They are mottled with yellow, white, and black, and have a yellow triangle on the lower third of each side. Young bugs (nymphs) are under 6.0 mm (0.25 in.), and greenish yellow, with five black dots. They are very shy and move very fast. Adults quickly fly away when approached. There are one or two broods a season. Adults hibernate in

weeds and trash in fall (see Figure 46, TARNISHED PLANT BUG).

THRIPS

Tiny translucent spots on rose petals, especially noticeable on clear white or very dark petals, are often formed by the minute thrips. They probe and suck the delicious rose petal juice. (This is very similar to a mosquito or flea sucking your blood.) A large number of these spots on petals renders a rose bloom useless. Swarms of thrips can cause rose buds to fail to open.

This tiny insect is up to 1 mm (0.04 in.) in length and about half the thickness of the letter "i" in this text. Its two pairs of wings are two thirds the length of the whole body, feathery and fold up neatly over the body when not in flight. Its flight is fast and movement on plants is quick and agile. Its mouth is equipped with a sucking probe like that of a mosquito. The insect is difficult to see because of its minute size and fast movement. When disturbed it prefers to fly rather than crawl. It is easiest to find and see by briskly tapping an infested blossom on your palm or a piece of white paper, and using a magnifying glass. Many broods are produced each year (see Figure 47, THRIP).

## Figure 48
## SLUG BAIT STATION

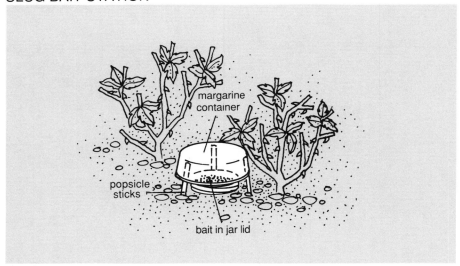

margarine container

popsicle sticks

bait in jar lid

### INSECT CONTROL

For the sake of convenience and simplicity, insects have been categorized according to the degree of difficulty in controlling them.

### EASY TO CONTROL INSECTS

Many of the common rose attacking insects are relatively easy to control. This group includes aphids, pear slugs, thrips, and rose curculio (weevil). A spray solution of the insecticides Malathion or Diazinon will control them. Dust insecticides such as Derris and Pyrethrum are also very effective but not long lasting and may require more frequent applications. Their main advantage is their relative safety feature of being non-poisonous to warm blooded animals.

### MODERATELY DIFFICULT INSECTS

More difficult insects to control are Tarnished Plant Bugs, Minute Pirate Bugs, Leafhoppers, and Leafcutter Bees. They are highly mobile and fly away when approached. A dust insecticide is most suitable as it remains on the plant until their return. A more lasting insecticide such as Diazinon or a systemic like Cygon or Cystox would also be effective.

The leafcutter bees are very sensitive to foreign substances on rose foliage and will, as a rule, avoid foliage with any chemical residue on it.

The insecticide-fungicide most often used by the author is a mixture of Funginex and Diazinon as recommended by the manufacturer. Many other formulations are also available such as LC-M Rosetox, Gardal, Pomogreen, or a number of Rose Dust formulations.

LC-M Rosetox is a U.S.A. product not presently available or registered for use in Canada (see RESOURCE MATERIALS).

### DIFFICULT INSECTS

Control of slugs is somewhat different and more difficult than for most insects. Insecticides commonly used for other insects are ineffective for slugs. I have seen some gardeners resort to table salt (sodium chloride) and lime. This will kill slugs but there is the danger that several applications each year and continued use of the mixture will seriously affect the quality and productivity of the soil. A more effective and safer method would be treatment with a slug bait containing Metaldehyde that is placed in protected bait or feeding stations. The stations are placed in shaded areas under the sheltering foliage of large plants and shrubs. These cafeteria type self-feeders may be purchased at garden centers.

Feeding stations may be made by using a coffee jar lid and an empty 200 gram plastic honey or margarine container (see Figure 48, SLUG BAIT STATION). The jar lid should be a bit smaller in diameter than the plastic container. The jar lid serves as a dish to hold the poison bait and the inverted plastic container provides the shelter to keep the bait dry and the location shady. Attach three popsicle sticks (evenly spaced) to the inside of the plastic container, and allow the sticks to protrude. Krazy Glue works well for attaching the sticks to the plastic container. Stick the legs of this container into the soil over the dish of bait allowing about 2 cm (0.75 in.) of crawl space. Inspect, clean and renew the poison bait every two or three days. The anchored container stays "put" in rain and wind. It also prevents birds and small pets from picking up the poison bait. Additional safeguards must be considered for larger cats and dogs. Be very careful if there are children about.

Some nurserymen scatter slug bait very lightly throughout their nursery a couple of times each week. This keeps their nursery slug-free. Some gardeners use 2% Mesurol bait at 500 g/100 m$^2$ (1 lb./1000 sq. ft.) scattered around where slugs are seen. Another method is spraying plants with a 20 percent Metaldehyde solution at 6 mL/L (2 Tbsp./gal.) of water.

A general clean-up, along with chemical use is necessary to obtain good control. Slugs' favorite shelter is tall un-cut grass, under board sidewalks, in woodpiles, and under debris lying on the ground. Removal of litter and mowing tall grass and weeds leaves them without adequate shelter.

### VERY DIFFICULT INSECTS

Red spider mites are the most persistent and perhaps the most difficult insect pest to control.

Spider mites flourish and multiply rapidly under dry, sunny conditions producing many generations a year. They abhor rain and damp conditions. People who are adverse to the use of chemicals use this fact to control them. Each week they spray the rose bushes with water being

Figure 49
BLACKSPOT

Blackspot first appears on the upper surface of the lower leaves of a rose bush as round black spots up to 12 mm (0.5 in.) in diameter. The leaves will soon yellow and drop off. The shrub rose, Persian Yellow, is very susceptible. Others vary from mildly susceptible to resistant to this disease (see Figure 49, BLACKSPOT).

Blackspot fungus spores over-winter on dead leaves or canes, and are spread by spores splashing up from the soil during watering or rainfall. If the fungus enters the leaf, its progress cannot be halted without destroying the leaf. An infected plant may lose all its leaves, then put out new ones, lose those and start leafing a third time. This drastically weakens the plant to the point where it may not survive the winter.

## BLACKSPOT FREE ROSES

Over the next few years a great variety of roses immune to blackspot will appear on the market. In 1979, a U.S.D.A. research scientist, Peter Semeniuk, developed three Hybrid Tea roses, Spotless Pink, Spotless Gold, and Spotless Yellow. The research administration has released budding material from these cultivars to amateur and commercial rose breeders in the U.S.A. Hopefully this work will be expanded and these roses will become available in Canada.

There are over fifty different strains of blackspot. Herein lies the difficulty for plant breeders trying to develop resistant cultivars.

## CROWN GALL

This bacterial disease appears as rough, roundish, tumor-like growths on rose canes near soil level. Infected plants lose vigor, become stunted and eventually die. The galls contain numerous bacteria, which can spread to other roses. Crown gall bacteria gain entry to plants through bruises and injury (see Figure 50, CROWN GALL).

Here is what many rose growers do to control this disease:

certain to wet the underside of the foliage. This manages to ward off spider mite damage, but it must be practiced religiously whenever spider mites or their damage is sighted.

Weekly spraying with a Malathion, Diazinon, or Cygon solution is also quite effective in spider mite control. Chemicals made specifically for spider mite control such as Pentac and Kelthane are also effective.

For non-chemical control, use Safer's Insecticidal Soap. It is an effective biodegradable contact insecticide which is safe to use on plants indoors or out. It is recommended for control of many insects on fruits, vegetables, trees, and shrubs. As it has no systemic action, spraying must be repeated. Many years before Safer's Insecticidal Soap was available, old-time gardeners used discarded soapy wash water on the garden and house plants to rid them of various pests. Later they turned to a more uniform solution by dissolving 4 tablespoons of Sunlight bar soap made into flakes or Ivory Soap flakes in 5 L (1 gal.) of water. Our grandmothers found it reasonably effective. However, the solution should be strained through a fine-mesh cloth; otherwise you'll have a clogged sprayer. Also, if the solution is left for a day or two, it has a tendency to

gel. The gel can be liquified by adding a bit of water and applying heat. In Safer's Insecticidal Soap you have a much more uniform product and no problem with sprayers or gelling.

"Avid", released last year for horticultural use in the U.S.A., is reported in the American Rose Magazine and Rose Ramblings Bulletin of the Spokane Rose Society to be the most effective chemical to date for the control of spider mites. "Avid" kills the adults and the eggs. The recommendation is to spray twice, one week apart, just to make certain that all spider mites and eggs are killed. Contact Agriculture Canada for information on importing pesticides (see RESOURCE MATERIALS).

## DISEASES

It has been said, "Almost anyone can grow roses in the spring. It is the summer, fall, and winter that separates the men from the boys." If you have reached mid-August and have had very few problems with insects and damage from disease, you are headed for success. The care given your roses from mid-August on ensures good growth and health to start off well the following year.

## FIGURE 50
## CROWN GALL

## Figure 51
## MILDEW

- Cyril C. Harris, in his book, "Beginners Guide to Rose Growing", recommends cutting away infected parts and painting with Bacticin (Published by Sphere Books Ltd., London).
- James Underwood Crockett (Time-Life Books, New York) in his book "Roses", recommends removal of galls and spraying with streptomycin, which may be obtained in spray or powder form at garden stores.
- Many gardeners have reported in the American Rose Society, and Spokane Rose Society monthly magazines that they have successfully used common household disinfectants such as Lysol, household bleach, and rubbing alcohol. The galls are removed and the wound painted with the disinfectant. Cutting tools are also treated to prevent the spread of bacteria.
- Before planting a new rose in infected soil, dip the roots in a Copper Fungicide solution.
- When a diseased bush has been removed, avoid planting roses in the infected area for three years.
- Another option when a diseased plant has been removed, is to remove the infected soil and replace it with fresh clean soil. It is considered sufficient to remove and replace up to 136 L (30 gal.) of soil from the area of the infected plant. The removed soil may be fumigated with formaldehyde and then replaced for planting. Complete instructions for disinfecting soil are given on containers of formaldehyde.
- Vapam, sodium methyldithiocarbamate can also be used to disinfect crown gall infested soil. It is not safe to use this product around live plants. The services of a licensed pesticide applicator will have to be obtained to use this product in some jurisdictions.
- Dig up the diseased rose bush and burn.
- Prevent water logging by providing adequate drainage. Crown Gall is rarely seen in roses grown in well drained, porous type soils.

### MILDEW

Mildew is a fungal disease appearing as greyish or white patches on tender rose parts including the buds. The patches resemble a layer of felt which gives the plant a frosty, powdery appearance. The leaves become stunted, thickened, and distorted. Stems are also stunted and the buds fail to open (see Figure 51, MILDEW).

Powdery mildew grows on the surface of both sides of leaves and invades the plant deeply. Its growth requires very little moisture. Cloudy days, moist nights, and poor air circulation are very conducive to the growth and spread of the disease.

### RUST

Rose rust first appears as small yellow pinprick marks on the upper surface of leaves low on a plant. Later, clusters of orange or black pustules appear on the underside of the leaf. Spores from these pustules are blown to other leaves and start new infections. Under cool, humid conditions these pustules may infect and eventually defoliate the bush. In early fall the pustules change color and become black. These overwinter in the leaf tissue to produce spores the following spring (see Figure 52, RUST).

### VIRAL DISEASES

Like most plants, roses are sometimes afflicted with various viral infections. They are spread mostly by biting and sucking insects, or by garden tools such as the hoe, cultivator, or pruner.

Figure 52
RUST

Figure 53
ROSE MOSAIC

## GENERAL CONTROL OF ROSE DISEASES

There are no chemical controls for viral diseases. Control is largely a matter of prevention. Nurserymen know this and strive to develop and maintain disease-free stock for their cuttings and bud-wood. Fortunately in Canada to date there have been no major problems with viral diseases in roses. If viral problems are suspected, they should be properly identified (provincial governments and/or universities usually offer this service).

A thorough cleanup of leaves and other debris reduces the places that insects and fungi can overwinter. Spraying the canes and the soil around rose bushes with a fungicide after the cleanup is a good practice.

Most fungal diseases thrive under warm, humid conditions. Therefore, avoid the use of overhead sprinklers and do not water in the evening, which would permit the rose to remain damp overnight.

Problems with blackspot, mildew, and rust can be controlled with a once-a-week spraying or dusting with fungicides such as Funginex, Captan, Benomyl, Phaltan, and Sulfur-Copper Dust.

The "Rose Hybridizers Newsletter", winter 1985, offers a non-toxic blackspot control from W.R. Shaw of Sydney, Australia. He sprays weekly with baking soda, using 6 mL/L (2 Tbsp./gal.) of water mixed with a spreader sticker. Shaw describes the formula as most effective against both blackspot and mildew. Shaw also uses, on occasion, a weekly spray of Lysol as a cure and preventative for mildew, mixed at the rate of 6 mL/L (1 oz./gal. of water).

### Rose Wilt

~~The most~~ A common viral disease is rose wilt. The whole plant or just a shoot may collapse and die. To prevent the spread of this disease, the entire plant or at least the infected portion should be removed and burned.

### Rose Mosaic

Another common virus is the rose mosaic /in some countries. However, it does not appear to hinder the plant's growth. When this virus becomes established, intricate yellow patterns are formed on the foliage (see Figure 53, ROSE MOSAIC).

Another formula for using baking soda as a control for mildew comes from Dr. Charles Jeremias in "The American Rose Society Magazine", December 1985. He recommends 2 mL/L (1.5 tsp./gal.) of water applied two days in a row.

Of the different fungicides available, the author chooses Funginex because it causes no leaf blemishes, and leaves no residues on the blossoms and foliage. Clear liquid solutions are preferable to dusts because they do not leave unsightly residues on the flowers and foliage.

If a combination fungicide-insecticide is desired to control fungal diseases and insects, any one of the following can be used:
- Gardal
- Pomogreen
- LC-M Rose Spray
- Ortho Rose Dust (Carbaryl, Malathion, Folpet, Dicofol)
- Green Cross Rose Dust (Carbaryl, Malathion, Captan, Sulfur)
- Chipman Rose Dust (Folpet, Malathion, Carbaryl).

## WEEDS

When you are fighting an enemy and expect to win, you must learn all about the enemy. You have to understand the enemy's weak points, and how and when to attack, otherwise you'll be the loser. Knowing the salient features of problem weeds will help you in controlling them. A starting point in understanding weed control is recognizing the various life cycles of the problem weeds, and capitalizing on the opportunities this presents. The problem weeds are categorized according to life cycle.

Perennials are plants that can generate growth from seed or root-stocks. They are capable of seed production, overwintering and continued growth, and spread for many years.

Many plants can behave as either annuals or winter annuals. These plants start their life cycle from seed. Those that start their life cycle early produce seed and die that same year. Others that start late do not produce seed in their first growing year, but overwinter and then continue their growth the following year to mature and produce seed.

Annuals complete their life cycle in a single growing season. Seedlings that start too late to mature seed are killed by frost in the fall.

## Figure 54
## CANADA THISTLE

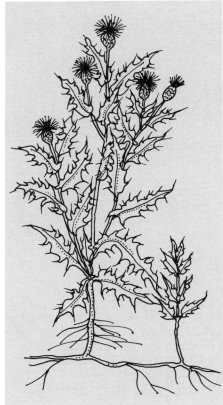

## PERENNIALS

### Canada Thistle

This plant has a very persistent, deep root system. Once established, a seedling will grow to take over a square metre (sq. yd.) in three years or less if no control is used. Stems grow up to 1.2 m (4 ft.), erect, with many branches; leaves are 5 - 13 cm (2 - 5 in.) long, deeply cut, and very prickly. Flowers are 2 - 2.5 cm (0.75 - 1 in.) in diameter, and vary from purple with a rose tinge to pink. Seeds are 3 mm (0.1 in.) long, dark green and attached to some fluff that is readily blown in the wind (see Figure 54, CANADA THISTLE).

### Perennial Sow Thistle

This is a light green perennial with deep root stocks that spread out readily like Canada Thistle. The hollow stems may grow up to 1.5 m (5 ft.) in height. Leaf margins have soft prickles and may grow up to 25 cm (10 in.) in length. Stems and

## Figure 55
## PERENNIAL SOW THISTLE

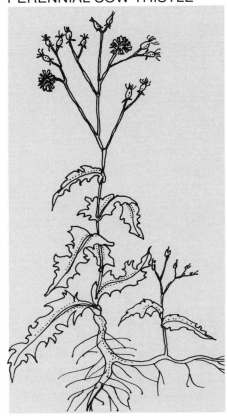

Figure 56
QUACK GRASS

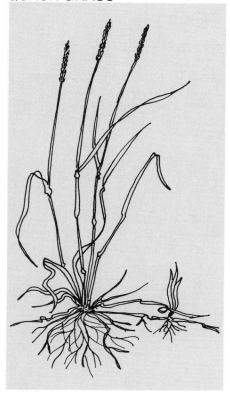

Figure 57
DANDELION

Figure 58
COMMON PLANTAIN

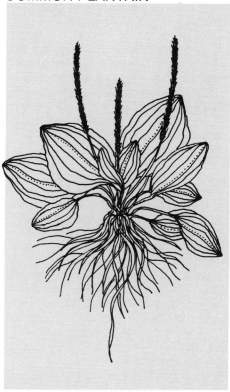

Figure 59
NARROW-LEAVED HAWK'S-BEARD

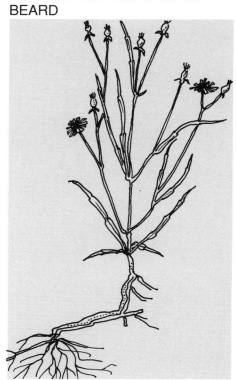

leaves exude a milky juice when broken. Bright yellow flowers are up to 4 cm (1.5 in.) in diameter and are grouped loosely on the ends of numerous stalks. The seeds are similar to that of Canada Thistle (see Figure 55, PERENNIAL SOW THISTLE).

### Quack (Couch) Grass

This is one of the worst of the grassy weeds. Quack grass spreads by seed and by underground, creeping stems called rhizomes. Rhizomes are whitish and tough with many nodes that produce new roots and stems. Stems are up to 1 m (3 ft.) or more tall. Leaves are rough on the surface and have a serrated margin. Flower spikes are green and 9.0 cm (3.5 in.) in length, and seed spikelets are 12 mm (0.5 in.) in length (see Figure 56, QUACK GRASS).

### Dandelion

One of the most common, persistent, and troublesome of garden weeds is the dandelion. There isn't a gardener who

doesn't know the dandelion. However, not many know that the deep fleshy root can sprout from root segments when cut up. This makes it difficult to eradicate by hoeing or other cultivation (see Figure 57, DANDELION).

### Common Plantain

This perennial plant has tough, tenacious roots that are not easy to pull out. The oval, strongly ribbed leaves are broad and spread out from the crown. Many grow up to 25 cm (10 in.) long. Flowers form a dense narrow spike on a leafless stem, about 7.5 - 30 cm (3 - 12 in.) long resembling a rifle brush. The spike produces numerous 3 mm (0.1 in.) long brown, egg-shaped seeds (see Figure 58, COMMON PLANTAIN).

### ANNUALS AND WINTER ANNUALS

### Narrow-leaved Hawk's-beard

This hollow-stemmed branching plant on first sight appears like a small slender Perennial Sow Thistle, including the milky juice when broken or bruised. The flowers are small and yellow and up to 2 cm (0.75 in.) across. Seeds are 3 mm (0.1 in.) long and attached to a bit of umbrella-like fluff that is easily disseminated throughout the garden. Juvenile plants are difficult to pull and often break off leaving the roots in position to regrow (see Figure 59, NARROW-LEAVED HAWK'S-BEARD).

### Stinkweed (Field Pennycress, Frenchweed)

This plant is easily recognized by its unpleasant odor when crushed. The stems are smooth and hairless, from 5 - 45 cm (2 - 18 in.) high, and may be single or branched. The leaves are smooth, hairless, and irregularly toothed. Flowers are small, white and 3 mm (0.1 in.) across, and form in clusters at the ends of stems. Seed pods are on slim upward curving stalks. They are oval, flat, and 8 - 12 mm (0.3 - 0.5 in.) across, and turn

Figure 60
STINKWEED

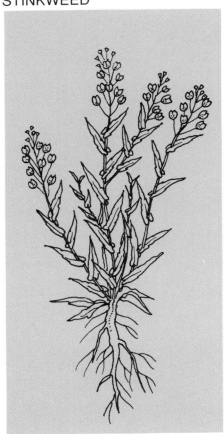

yellow when ripe. Seeds are 2 mm (0.1 in.) in diameter, and a reddish brown to black. Seeds have been known to remain viable in the soil for 30 years (see Figure 60, STINKWEED).

### Shepherd's Purse

This weed is only spread by seeds. The stems may be single or branched and up to 50 cm (20 in.) high or more. Leaves are slightly hairy; the basal leaves form a rosette and are deeply cut and lobed. Flowers are small, white, and about 2 - 3 mm (0.1 in.) wide, in terminal racemes. Seed pods are triangular and notched at top, and are 6 mm (0.25 in.) long on spreading stalks from 0.5 - 2 cm (0.2 - 0.8 in.) long. Seeds are 1 mm (0.05 in.) long. It is a very persistent weed in

Figure 61
SHEPHERD'S PURSE

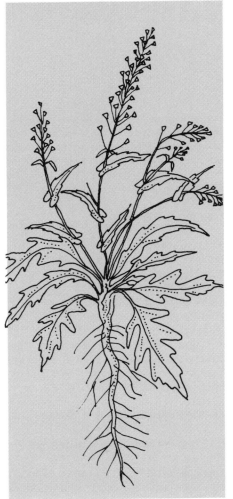

gardens (see Figure 61, SHEPHERD'S PURSE).

ANNUALS

### Common Chickweed

Normally, this weed behaves as an annual. Occasionally, plants will survive the winter in protected areas. It is one of

Figure 62
COMMON CHICKWEED

Figure 63
ANNUAL POA

the most troublesome weeds in the garden. Usually chickweed grows prostrate or trailing with a line of fine hairs on one side of the stem. The leaves are 6 mm - 2.5 cm (0.25 - 1 in.) long. Flowers are white, 6 mm (0.25 in.) long, and star-shaped, with 5 petals. Seeds are in a small capsule, are very small like fine pepper, and very numerous (see Figure 62, COMMON CHICKWEED).

## Annual Poa

This is a short-lived annual grassy weed. It is related to other perennial Blue Grasses except that its leaves are pale green and very soft. It grows in clumps that are easy to pull. It is a prolific seed producer, which makes it a nuisance in the home garden. It germinates at any time during the summer especially when the soil is damp. This habit makes it tough to eradicate. This grass does not survive the winter (see Figure 63, ANNUAL POA).

## Purslane

This prostrate, fleshy-leafed weed, is troublesome in gardens. The stems are reddish and may be up to 30 cm (1 ft.) tall. Flowers are small, yellow and appear in clusters at the end of stems and in leaf axils. It is a prolific seed producer, and the seeds may remain viable in the soil for several years. This makes it difficult to control. Packages of mixed flower seeds are common sources of infestation. Purslane will readily re-establish itself if left on the soil surface after cultivating or hoeing. Plants must be completely removed and destroyed if control is to be successful (see Figure 64, PURSLANE).

## Corn Spurry

This plant grows with several stems 15 - 45 cm (6 - 18 in.) high, forming at the base. The stems are a little hairy and sticky. Leaves are very narrow, 2.5 - 4 cm (1 - 1.5 in.) long and curving upward in clusters. Flowers are white, about 6 mm (0.25 in.) across and attached to the top of the stems by thin stalks. It is a prolific seed producer with seeds germinating at any time during the summer (see Figure 65, CORN SPURRY).

## Common Groundsel

The stems are hollow, usually branched, and 15 - 40 cm (6 - 16 in.) high; leaves are lobed and toothed. Flowers come in clusters at the end of the branches. They are 6 mm (0.25 in.) across and yellow. The small seeds are attached to a fluffy fuzz, which permits them to be easily carried by the wind. The seeds germinate at any time during the summer making them a constant pest in the garden. Mature plants are difficult to pull and most often break off just above ground level (see Figure 66, COMMON GROUNDSEL).

## Lamb's Quarters (Pigweed)

This plant will grow anywhere from a few centimetres (1 in.) up to nearly a metre (3 ft.). The stems are branched, ridged, and sometimes have reddish lines. Leaves have wavy margins, and the lower surface is a soft grey-green and coated with powdery, mealy particles. Flowers are small, greenish colored, and without petals. They are arranged in dense panicles in leaf axils and at the top of the plant. Seeds are 1 mm (0.05 in.) across,

Figure 64
PURSLANE

Figure 65
CORN SPURRY

Figure 66
COMMON GROUNDSEL

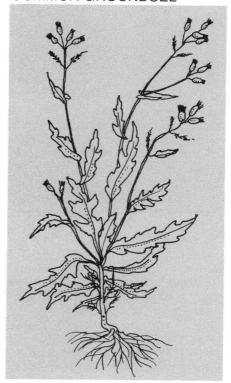

Figure 67
LAMB'S QUARTERS

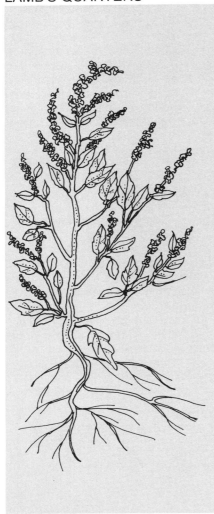

Figure 68
GREEN FOXTAIL

Figure 69
RED-ROOT PIGWEED

Figure 70
PINEAPPLEWEED

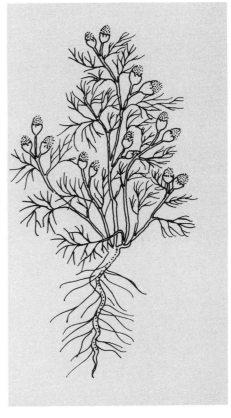

shiny, black, flat, and almost round. It is a very common weed that is often introduced through packaged garden seeds or barnyard manure. As with many weeds, the seeds may remain viable in the soil for many years (see Figure 67, LAMB'S QUARTERS).

### Green Foxtail (Wild Millet)

The stems of Green Foxtail may be simple or branched, and anywhere from a few centimetres (1 in.) up to a metre (3 ft.) tall depending on the density of the infestation. Leaves are short and broader than most grasses, and look a little like corn as seedlings. Flower spikes may be 2.5 - 10 cm (1 - 4 in.) long, and resemble a rifle cleaner. Green Foxtail produces a prolific number of small seeds about 2 mm (0.1 in.) long. It can become a troublesome weed in the garden. A common source of infestation is packaged garden seeds, especially carrots. Plants are easy to pull or hoe making this type of control the recommended practice (see Figure 68, GREEN FOXTAIL).

### Red-Root Pigweed

This annual weed is easily identified by its red or pink taproot. Stems are erect, rough, slightly hairy at the tip, and grow up to 75 cm (30 in.) tall. Leaves are long-stalked, alternate, ovate, slightly hairy, dull green in color, and 7.5 - 10 cm (3 - 4 in.) long. Flowers are green in dense spikes in leaf axils and on the terminal spike at the top of the plant. Seeds are 1 mm (0.05 in.) in diameter, almost round, and a glossy jet black. They can lay dormant in the soil for many years, and will germinate when conditions are favorable (see Figure 69, RED-ROOT PIGWEED).

### Pineappleweed

This annual looks very much like many of the mayweeds, but has a pleasant pineapple fragrance when crushed. It grows 7.5 - 40 cm (3 - 16 in.) high. The leaves are divided several times. Pineappleweed flowers are 6 mm (0.25 in.) across with yellow center florets but no ray flowers (visible petals). It is a prolific seed producer that can become a persistent weed in gardens (see Figure 70, PINEAPPLEWEED).

## CHEMICAL WEED CONTROL

Home or hobby gardeners who do not produce commercially need to recognize that chemical weed control in areas other than lawns is generally not for them. Chemical weed control is a complex operation in small areas in the vicinity of sensitive plants. A hobby gardener may not have proper equipment and will often find it difficult to apply the correct rate of herbicide on a small scale. Individuals who know how to use herbicides make a point of keeping up-to-date on the numerous weed control chemicals and their uses. In garden weed control, chemicals must be used with extreme caution.

In spite of the cautions already stated, there are chemicals that can be used very effectively for controlling certain weeds in certain areas. Such cases include the following:
- If you wish to establish a rose garden in an area infested with Canadian Thistle, Quack Grass, or other persistent perennials, you can do so with Round-Up (glyphosate). Used according to instructions on the label, Round-Up will eliminate weeds and render the soil suitable for cultivation and growing roses in about 10 days. The weeds must be actively growing at the time of chemical application.
- Perennial weeds growing in the rose bed may be treated individually by painting their foliage with a prepared solution of Round-Up using a small paint brush. Care should be taken not to get the chemical on the roses.

## CULTURAL WEED CONTROL

Most rose gardeners rely on cultural weed control methods that include mulching, hoeing, cultivating, and hand weeding.

Mulch may be any organic material such as decomposed manure, peat moss, compost, chopped weed-free straw or hay, or lawn clippings if free from herbicides. A mulch 5 - 8 cm (2 - 3 in.) thick will retard weed growth, conserve moisture, and maintain a uniform soil temperature. In time, the mulch decomposes and becomes part of the organic matter thereby enriching the soil.

To keep ahead of the weeds, hoe or cultivate when the weeds are small, under 5 cm (2 in.), and the soil surface is dry. Frequent hoeings are much easier and effective than wrestling tough, large weeds from the soil. Cultivation should be shallow so that the roots of the roses are not damaged.

## ANIMAL PEST CONTROL

The most common animal pests damaging roses are deer, rabbits, and field mice.

Deer and rabbits are not common urban pests but they can be troublesome in rural areas. They can be kept out of your roses in one of three ways:
- Build an adequate fence or screen that will keep these animals out of the garden.
- Have a dog around to discourage these animals from coming near the garden.
- Spray the plants with a repellent such as "Skoot" or any similar product. This product is generally used in fall to protect plants during winter and early spring.

Field mice can be a problem in urban or rural areas. They do the greatest damage to roses during the winter, particularly when there is a deep snow cover over long grasses, weeds, or straw mulches. Mice tunnel under the snow along the ground and chew the bark off roses and other sweet tasting shrubs and trees. You may also see mouse damage at the snow surface level. To control mice in and around the garden, build V-troughs made out of two pieces of lumber 1 m (3 ft.) long, and 2.5 x 10 cm (1 x 4 in.) and 2.5 x 12.5 cm (1 x 5 in.) wide. The wider board is nailed onto the edge of the narrow board. Invert the V-troughs and place a small tin lid filled with poison mouse bait beneath the boards. Make several of these and place them strategically in your garden among the shrubs just before snowfall. Mice like to crawl and hide in the protected areas that these bait stations provide. Exercise considerable caution where children or pets have access to the bait stations (see Figure 71, MOUSE BAIT STATION).

## Figure 71
## MOUSE BAIT STATION

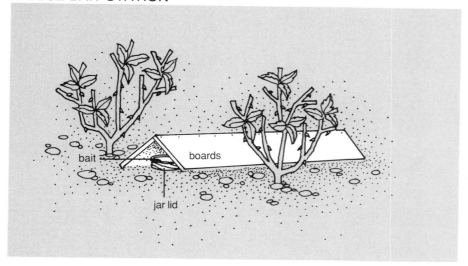

bait

boards

jar lid

## TRADE NAMES

In this publication wherever trade names appear for products, they are used only to identify the chemicals as they are known in the market place. No endorsement is intended nor discrimination implied against products not mentioned or listed.

# SHOWING AND DISPLAYING ROSES

## TYPES OF DISPLAY OR STAGING

Roses can be exhibited in many ways. Here are a few representative classes selected from various show schedules:

- Single stem, one bloom
- Hybrid Tea - fully open (fully blown)
- Vase of roses
- Collection of five Hybrid Teas
- Collection of different types of roses
- Bowl - single specimen
- Bowl - arrangement
- English Box - six specimen bloom
- Rose arrangement
- Rose Bouquet
- Corsage and Boutonniere
- Cycle of Bloom
- Potted miniature rose
- Miniature English box
- Miniature Rose - one bloom
- Miniature Rose - one spray
- Grandiflora Rose - one spray (could be divided to accommodate various colors)
- Floribunda Rose - one spray (could be divided to accommodate various colors)

This is not a definitive list, but merely indicates some of the very many classes possible. The descriptions that follow are intended to illustrate some of the important considerations in the various classes. Check the show regulations, ask questions of organizers, and see the RESOURCE MATERIALS section for more information.

### SINGLE STEM, ONE BLOOM

This class is generally used for Hybrid Teas, Grandifloras, and miniatures.

Unless the single specimen class at the show calls for fully open blooms, double bloom roses look best when they are 1/2 - 3/4 open; single and semi-double blooms when fully open (see Figure 72, SINGLE STEM, ONE BLOOM).

Figure 72
SINGLE STEM, ONE BLOOM

Full bloom is the stage when all petals are symmetrically unfurled and arranged within a circular outline. **Buds are not suitable as rose show specimens**. A bud is considered to be a bud up to the stage of development where it is beginning to show full color, with only one or two petals commencing to unfurl above an opening calyx.

One bloom specimens should have stems to complement the bloom. In most cases, it is a stem with at least two sets of five or more leaflets. The exhibitor should not be too overly concerned if the stem does not come up to this rigid specification, as long as the foliage is pleasing to the eye and has proper balance and proportion.

Single specimen rose exhibits are shown with no side buds. These should be removed when very small so that it does not show any signs of removal or scars. It is best done at least 20 days before the show.

Beware of stem-on-stem specimens. These are created when secondary growth appears after the primary stem has been cut. A bloom on a secondary stem branching from the cut primary stem is called Stem-on-Stem (see Figure 73, STEM-ON-STEM). **This is not permitted at rose shows and will be disqualified**.

Figure 73
STEM-ON-STEM

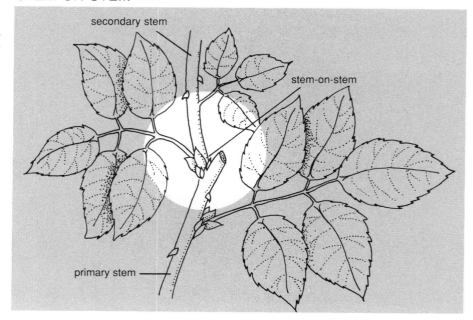

secondary stem

stem-on-stem

primary stem

### HYBRID TEA – FULLY OPEN

Fully open roses in this class have blossoms with petals completely unfurled, and blossoms with fewer petals, stamens showing.

### VASE OF ROSES

This class calls for either three to five or more long-stemmed roses in a vase. Show rules may call for one color only, harmonious colors, or different colors. Make sure you use a regulation container (check the show rules). Remove lower thorns and leaves—those which may be inside the container.

### COLLECTION OF FIVE HYBRID TEAS

Usually five different cultivars are used and exhibited in individual containers. Try to have blooms of uniform size with stems the same length.

### COLLECTION OF DIFFERENT TYPES OF ROSES

This class is to show the different types of roses available: for example, Hybrid Tea, Grandiflora, Floribunda, Polyantha, and Miniature.

### BOWL – SINGLE SPECIMEN

A fully open bloom is floated on a rose leaf or two in about 2.5 cm (1 in.) of water in a bowl (large blooms are best for this). The stem is cut very short so that the bloom rests flat on the leaf on top of the water (see Figure 74, BOWL - SINGLE SPECIMEN).

### BOWL – ARRANGEMENT

Specimens for this class require medium length stems. Each bloom in this bowl arrangement must be clear of its neighbor. Do not allow blooms to touch each other and yet avoid having large gaps between them (see Figure 75, BOWL - ARRANGEMENT).

### ENGLISH BOX

These boxes are specially built to facilitate exhibiting 6, 9, 12, 15, 18 or 24 short-stemmed roses. The larger blossoms are placed in the back tubes. The most popular in Canada and the U.S.A. is the box of six. No foliage is required. This type of exhibit is popular with gardeners who do not have the well-foliaged, long-stemmed, "regal" type roses. The flower size should be uniform, and the degree of openness is important

— preferably 2/3 - 3/4 open. The color of each flower should complement the others in the box if possible. A regular size box for six blooms is 19 x 37 cm (7.5 x 14.5 in.), and 2.5 cm (1 in.) higher at one end than the other (see Figure 76, ENGLISH BOX).

### ROSE ARRANGEMENT

This class is generally left to the exhibitor's imagination, ingenuity, and good taste. Show rules will give specifics as to foliage permitted and the occasion for which it is intended (see Figure 77, ROSE ARRANGEMENT).

### ROSE BOUQUET

A rose bouquet consists of anywhere from 6 - 12 long-stemmed roses of a single color, or a pleasing, harmonious combination of colors. The stems must be of equal length. There is no special arrangement required for this exhibit.

### CORSAGE AND BOUTONNIERE

Small Hybrid Tea type blossoms are excellent for corsages and boutonnieres (see Figure 78, CORSAGE). The cultivar Faberge continues to win many awards in this class. The flowers are long-lasting,

Figure 74
BOWL - SINGLE SPECIMEN

Figure 75
BOWL - ARRANGEMENT

Figure 76
ENGLISH BOX

Figure 77
ROSE ARRANGEMENT

Figure 78
CORSAGE

Figure 79
CYCLE OF BLOOM

Figure 80
MINI ENGLISH BOX

beautifully sculptured, slightly fragrant, and excellent in form, both in the bud and fully open stages. Also very good for the petite corsage is the Polyantha, light pink colored rose, Cecile Brunner. For a boutonniere, a rose just starting to open,

with sepals down, all color showing, and petals still unfurling is ideal in this class.

### CYCLE OF BLOOM

The cycle of bloom should show three stages of bloom of the same cultivar of a Hybrid Tea type; one bud, one show form bloom, and one full bloom. The bud should have the color just beginning to show, sepals down, and petals just starting to unfurl. The show form bloom should be 1/2 - 3/4 open depending on the number of petals in the bloom (the more petals, the more open it should be). The fully blown bloom must show stamens (see Figure 79, CYCLE OF BLOOM).

### POTTED MINIATURE ROSE

The pot for the miniature rose should not exceed 20 - 22 cm (8 - 9 in.). Check the rules and prize schedule closely as this could vary from show to show. There may be a class for a potted, miniature standard rose as well.

### MINIATURE ENGLISH BOX

In all respects this class is the same as the regular English Box except for size.

The same rules apply as to uniformity of size, degree of openness, color match, and harmony. The box should measure 10 x 18 cm (4 x 7 in.) (see Figure 80, MINI ENGLISH BOX).

### MINIATURE ROSE – ONE BLOOM

Miniature roses reflect the form, color, substance, and size of all the types of the larger Hybrid Teas. In form they have a greater variation and are judged on their own individual merits. The point scoring system is the same as for the Hybrid Teas.

### MINIATURE ROSE – ONE SPRAY

The miniature spray is judged on the same basis as set for judging Floribunda roses.

### GRANDIFLORA ROSE – ONE SPRAY

The objective in a Grandiflora spray is to create a mass display of blooms at the same stage of development. All things being equal, a cultivar showing mass blooming should win over one showing various stages of bloom. When the first bud is removed, most Grandifloras produce blooms in mass effect. This is more the accepted ideal, with flower form also getting important consideration. The spray should show two or more blooms.

## FLORIBUNDA ROSE – ONE SPRAY

Floribundas are judged on the basis of showing the various stages of development. Ideally, the Floribunda inflorescence should show all stages of development from green buds to those beginning to unfurl, 1/3 open, 1/2 open, 3/4 open and fully open. Some cultivars, because of their characteristics, open to the same stage of development at the same time, usually full blown. Other cultivars exhibit two stages, bud and full blown. For maximum score, the number of mature flowers should be more in evidence than the buds and less developed florets. The overall appearance of the inflorescence, rather than the form of each individual bloom, is of prime importance (see Figure 81, SPRAY OF FLORIBUNDA ROSES).

## Figure 81
## SPRAY OF FLORIBUNDA ROSES

# JUDGE'S POINT SYSTEM

This scoring system allocates values to the various rose attributes. It is mainly used when tight decisions have to be made. The point system is also used to average a score when more than one judge is evaluating an exhibit.

An exhibitor must be aware that the point system is not used by the judge in a formal way for every rose judged. That would take hours to complete. However, it gives a novice judge an idea of the relative values of the various components. The point scoring system also assists rose exhibitors in meeting the criteria.

**FORM:** 25 points

This is the most valuable attribute in an exhibition rose. Generally, the most perfect phase of beauty is when a rose is 1/2 - 3/4 open. It must be symmetrical, with a circular outline. It must have a sufficient number of petals, gracefully shaped, and appear to be high centered. Roses which are in most perfect phase when 1/2 - 2/3 open (fewer petalled cultivars) should have at least 3 - 4 rows of petals unfurling. Blooms with somewhat more petals are in perfect phase when 1/2 - 2/3 open with 3 - 4 rows of petals unfurling.

Blooms with a larger number of petals should be slightly more open (2/3 - 3/4 ), and have at least 4 - 5 rows of petals unfurling.

The bud stage of growth continues to the point where the sepals are down, petals just beginning to unfurl, and the configuration of the center is not evident. A bud is not a bloom and cannot be considered for any award for a bloom.

The decorative type Hybrid Teas vary somewhat from the standard Hybrid Teas in that they may **not** have a well-defined high and pointed center. It may be ruffled, cupped, and can have a low, sunken rather than pointed center. Otherwise they have identical judging standards.

Single Hybrid Tea roses have from 5 - 12 petals. They are most perfect when fully opened. They may be shown as one bloom or as a spray.

**COLOR:** 20 points

Color is composed of the hue, chroma, and brightness. Hue is the factor that gives visual impact to the eye and distinguishes one color from another. Chroma is the purity and intensity of the hue. Brightness is the clarity of the hue (free of cloudiness).

Rose Judging Standards list the following color classes (the small letters following the color is the abbreviation for the color often used in rose literature):
- White or near white - w
- Medium yellow - my
- Deep yellow - dy
- Yellow blend - yb
- Apricot blend - ab
- Orange - o
- Orange blend - ob
- Orange red - or
- Light pink - lp
- Medium pink - mp
- Deep pink - dp
- Pink blend - pb
- Medium red - mr
- Dark red - dr
- Red blend - rb
- Mauve - m
- Russet - r

There are also the bi-colors. These roses have one color when viewed from the top, but show a different color on the reverse side of the petal. Good examples of this are:
- Oriana - red with a white reverse
- Miss Canada - pink with a silvery-white reverse.

**STEM AND FOLIAGE:** 20 points

The stem should be straight, the proper length, not too coarse or too thin, and with typical thorns. The foliage should be undamaged, clean, well groomed, of sufficient number, and of proper size. **A stem-on-stem specimen is disqualified.**

Disbudding should be done at an early stage so that the resulting scar will be as small as possible and not too noticeable.

A stem with two (three leaflet) leaves above three (five, seven, or nine leaflet) leaves generally presents a complete specimen.

**SUBSTANCE: 15 points**

Substance is rated as the keeping quality of the rose. It is constituted by texture, crispness, firmness, thickness, and toughness of the petals. Loss of substance is first evident by a faint browning and discoloring of the edges of the outer petals.

**BALANCE AND PROPORTION: 10 points**

The balance and proportion of a rose refers to the overall pleasing appearance of the specimen. This is judged by how the bloom relates to the stem and foliage, and how the bloom, stem, and foliage complement each other (one being not too large or too small for the other).

**SIZE: 10 points**

This actually refers to the proper size of the bloom. All other things being equal, correct size can become the determining factor in placing one specimen over another. A bloom that is clearly undersized or oversized will receive a small penalty.

## HINTS ON SHOWING ROSES

Grandifloras, Floribundas, Polyanthas and climbers are exhibited as clusters or trusses of flowers on a single stem. Buds are permitted in the cluster. The overall form of the spray can take the shape of a circle, oval or any other geometric form pleasing to the eye. From the side, the spray can take on a flat appearance, with all the florets on the same level, or a domed appearance. To present a good appearance, spent blooms and unwanted growth may be removed if done without impairing the exhibit.

All roses must be named correctly. Variety name is stressed and judges disqualify blooms that are without labels

or are incorrectly named. Rose shows enable gardeners to select cultivars to try in their own garden.

Crooked stems can be straightened by tying the stem to a stake in at least three different places about two weeks before the show (see Figure 24, STAKING ROSES). The leaves will take their normal position to the sun in that time.

For show purposes, it is essential that the rose be clean and free of chemical residue, dust, disease, and insects. Foliage may be cleaned by wiping with a moist, soft flannel cloth. Other foreign material on the bloom can be removed with a camel's hair brush.

To have the rose specimen show some freshness, it is necessary to cut it as close to show time as possible. Cutting and preserving roses is important. Please refer to sections on BASIC PRUNING and KEEPING CUT FLOWERS for additional information.

Occasionally, you may have a bloom that is opening in a lopsided manner. It can be manipulated into proper shape by careful use of a soft camel's hair brush. Begin by carefully manipulating the brush inside the outer row, then into the next row of petals as required. To do this effectively, practice on several blooms not intended for showing. Before using the brush try blowing into the bloom. The warm air blast at times is all that is necessary to open it up. The camel's hair brush can also be used to open up a bloom that may be too tight for exhibition.

Tips of petals that have been bruised or torn may be skilfully sheared away with sharp manicure scissors. A damaged leaf can similarly be manicured. Done with care, the damaged part will hardly be noticeable.

A single prized bloom can be protected from rain or hot sun by placing a styrofoam cup over it. Do not let the cup touch the bloom (see Figure 82, PROTECTING BLOOMS FROM WEATHER). The cup is adjusted to the proper height by sticking the wire end into the ground. A Twist-tie wrapped

**Figure 82**
**PROTECTING BLOOMS FROM WEATHER**

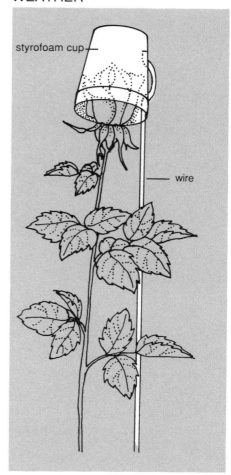

styrofoam cup

wire

around the rose cane and wire will keep the cup from vibrating and rubbing the bloom during a wind storm.

Waxing or oiling of foliage does not improve the appearance. Rose foliage is best when exhibited in its natural healthy state. Whether foliage is glossy or mat-textured depends on the variety.

## ROSE BLOOM FAULTS

The following are common faults that rose exhibitors must avoid:
- Too many or too few petals result in a form not typical for the variety.
- Petals not regularly arranged to form a circular outline when viewed from the top and the bloom lacks symmetry.

Figure 83
CONFUSED CENTER

- A split or confused center is a faulty arrangement of petals in the center of the bloom, giving the appearance of a double center (see Figure 83, CONFUSED CENTER). A prominent split is much more serious than one that is just beginning to be obvious.
- Dwarfed and distorted blooms and buds caused by mildew, excess rain, and insects are also faulted.

## KEEPING CUT FLOWERS

The proper way of cutting and handling roses can add days of life to your display flowers.

Use a very sharp knife—the cleaner the cut, the better the stem is able take up water. Most florists prefer a slant cut because it creates a greater area for water absorption. Dull cutting instruments have a tendency to crush the stem end, which reduces water uptake.

Place your cut roses in a bucket or other container as they are cut. Use a bucket that has been cleaned thoroughly. Any bacteria or fungi in the container can grow rapidly and soon kill your flowers. Some people use aspirin, copper pennies, sugar and soft drinks in the flower vases. These may be harmful if used without a bactericide or fungicide. They stimulate the growth of bacteria and fungi that clog the water conducting tissue in the stem. It is better to invest your time and money in a good floral preservative such as Petal Lite, Rose Life, Bloom Life, or Floralife. It is difficult to keep bacteria and fungi out of water without a preservative. Changing the water every day helps, but it will not eliminate microbial growth. De-ionized or boiled water is much better for cut flowers than tap water. Cut plants take in several times the amount of de-ionized or boiled water than tap water.

The best time to cut roses is when the temperature is cool — in the evening or early morning. Take your bucket with warm water (40° C or 100 - 110° F) with preservative to the garden where you are cutting. Place the cut flowers immediately into this solution. Any delay here will cause air to enter the water conducting tissue in the cut end. This will prevent water from being taken up by the plant. Re-cutting under water will guarantee that no air is taken in. Hold the roses in a warm solution for 1 - 2 hours. This helps the flowers to quickly absorb water. Following this, place them in cool, "preservative spiked", de-ionized water in a cool dark place for 4 - 8 hours. This is called "conditioning".

Following the conditioning, roses may be refrigerated at around 1 - 2° C (34 - 36° F), or they may be displayed or arranged. Again, take the same precautions by using clean vases, bowls, de-ionized water, preservative, and a fresh cut on each stem. The foliage below the water level should be stripped. Leaves under water start decaying very rapidly. This procedure will double the life of cut roses, so it is well worth the effort. Cut flowers and foliage deterioration is ten times faster at 20° C (70° F) than at 0° C (32° F).

Cutting roses at the proper stage of maturity is important. If cut when buds are too tight, they will never open. If left too long, they may be past their prime. A good time to cut them is when two or three outer petals are starting to unfold. To keep roses from opening too fast, wrap a piece of paper loosely around the bloom, hold in place with tape, and keep refrigerated at around 1 - 2° C (34 - 36° F).

Do not keep fruit in a refrigerator when you are storing roses in it. The gas given off by the ripening fruit has a damaging effect on roses.

## RESTORING WILTED ROSES

Wilted cut roses can be revived and made to look quite presentable. Immerse the roses, leaves and all, in 40° C water in a bathtub. Cut 2.5 cm (1 in.) of their stem ends under water. Make sure the stems and necks are straightened or they will come out firm but bent. One hour under water will straighten them out and make them look fresh again.

## TRANSPORTING ROSES

Transporting roses can present serious problems. Cut roses should not be exposed to sun, wind, heat, or extreme cold. Roses can be taken for a considerable distance in one of several ways:

- Wrap each rose separately in a soft, florist waxed paper and lay them in a box with a roll of newspaper for a neck pillow. Place plastic bags of ice at the base of stems and fasten securely.

- Rose specimens can be transported long distances in long individual tubes with some water in the base.
- Each rose can be wrapped separately as described previously and placed into a partially filled pail of iced water.

# LEARNING MORE ABOUT ROSES

## ROSE SOCIETIES

A lot of information and assistance can be obtained from the publications and fellow members of the various Rose Societies.

In addition to the annual publications they produce each year, Rose Societies also publish magazines. These manuals and magazines provide informative articles written by experts on current developments in the world of roses, and practical tips on growing and showing roses. You may also have access to a slide library of roses, and lists of shows and rose gardens for your personal pleasure.

The three major societies of interest to Canadians are:
- Canadian Rose Society
  C/O Mrs. Bea Hunter
  20 Portico Drive
  Scarborough, Ont.
  M1G 3R3
  Membership: $15.00 per year

- American Rose Society
  P.O. Box 30,000
  Shreveport, Louisiana 71130
  U.S.A.
  Membership: $25.00 per year
  (in U.S. Funds)

- Royal National Rose Society
  Chiswell Green Lane
  St. Albans, Herts, England
  AL2 3NR
  Membership: £8 per year

## JOIN A ROSE OR HORTICULTURAL SOCIETY

At meetings and shows you meet many who are knowledgeable about rose growing. Their knowledge is helpful especially if you are just starting to grow roses or are new to the district. At the shows you see the roses you like the best and meet the people who grow them.

In the Spokane Rose Society publication, "Rose Ramblings", September 1985, the editor wrote: "Smart rosarians learn by the mistakes of others. You don't have time to make all of them yourself!"

## ORDER AND PERUSE THE LATEST ROSE CATALOGUES

Write the rose nurseries for their catalogues and study them. They contain valuable information and numerous helpful suggestions.

## SUBSCRIBE TO THE "COMBINED LIST"

This manual is published and updated annually. It lists:
- Roses in commerce and cultivation.
- Rose registrations update.
- Hard-to-find roses and where to find them.
It is published by:
  Beverly R. Dobson
  215 Harriman Road
  Irvington, N.Y., 10533
  U.S.A.
  Price: $10.00 U.S.

## VISIT ROSE GARDENS

See for yourself how rose growers manage to grow their roses. Each rosarian has his own particular way of doing things and has to overcome different problems. This is the best way to learn the art of growing roses.

To encourage this idea, in 1986, the Canadian Rose Society obtained the consent of selected members throughout Canada to open their rose gardens for public viewing. The author feels honored that his rose garden had been chosen for Alberta.

# RESOURCE MATERIALS

## IMPORTING ROSES

Outlined below is the proper procedure for ordering rose bushes from a foreign country:

1. Make up an order from the catalogue of the company you wish to import from.

2. Obtain an import permit, stating the number of rose bushes and the nursery ordered from. To obtain a permit in Alberta write to:
   - Agriculture Canada
     Plant Protection Division
     820 Federal Public Bldg.
     9820 - 107 St.
     Edmonton, Alberta T5K 1E7
   or
   - Agriculture Canada
     Plant Protection Division
     1415 1st St. S.E.
     Calgary, Alberta T2G 2J3

   In Saskatchewan the address is:
   - Agriculture Canada
     Plant Protection Division
     817 Motherwell
     Regina, Sask. S4P 3R4

   In Manitoba write to:
   - Agriculture Canada
     Plant Protection Division
     722 Federal Blvd.
     269 Main St.
     Winnipeg, Man. R3C 1B2

   To obtain import information for other areas of Canada, write to:
   - Agriculture Canada
     Plant Protection Division
     960 Carling Ave
     Ottawa, Ont. K1A 0C6

3. With the permit, you will receive permit labels from the Plant Protection Division. Send these permit labels and your rose order to the nursery. They will use these labels on the package when sending your roses. The package will arrive through Canadian Quarantine and Customs Office in your name.

## MAIL ORDER SUPPLIERS

- Armstrong Nurseries
  P.O. Box 1020
  Somis, CA. 93066
  U.S.A.
  Phone: 1 - 800 - 321-6640

- Byland's Nurseries Ltd.
  1600 Byland Rd.
  Kelowna, B.C. V1Z 1H6
  Phone: (604) 769-4466

- Carl Pallek & Son Nurseries
  Box 137
  Virgil, Ontario L0S 1T0
  Phone: (416) 468-7262

- Hortico Inc.
  723 Robson Rd. R.R. 1
  Waterdown, Ont. L0R 2H0
  Phone: (416) 689-6984

- Jackson & Perkins Co.
  1 Rose Lane
  Medford, OR. 97501
  U.S.A.

- LeGrice Roses
  Norwich Road North Walsham
  Norfolk, England NR2 0DR
  (minimum order: £20)

- Morden Nurseries Ltd.
  P.O. Box 1020
  Morden, Manitoba R0G 1J0
  Phone: (204) 822-3311

- Pickering Nurseries
  670 Kingston Rd. (Hwy 2)
  Pickering, Ontario L1V 1A6
  Phone: (416) 839-2111

- R. Harkness & Co. Ltd.
  The Rose Gardens, Hitchin
  Herts, England SG4 0JT

- W. Kordes' Sohne
  Rosenstrasse 54
  2206 Klein Offenseth
  Sparrieshoop in Holstein
  West Germany

## PLANS FOR THE SUPER WEEDER

Order from:
University of Alberta
Faculty of Extension
Room 238, Corbett Hall
Edmonton, Alberta T6G 2G4
Price: $2.00

## INSECTICIDES, FUNGICIDES

Listed below are rose chemicals that are presently not registered or available in Canada. In time, our foremost garden supply shops will have them. (There may be restrictions on the use of certain chemicals. Check your federal regulations.)

LC-M Rosetox is available in the U.S.A. from Bonide Chemical Co., Inc., Dept. AR-2, Wurz Avenue, Yorkville, NY 13495.

Avid Miticide is available in the U.S.A. through dealers of the manufacturer: MSD Agvet, Division of Merck & Co., Inc., P.O. Box 2000, Rahway, New Jersey 07065. One of their dealers is Kimbrew-Walter Roses, Route 2, Box 172, Grand Saline, Texas 75140, Phone (214) 829-2968.

## USEFUL REFERENCE BOOKS

A.R.S. *A Rose Buying Guide.* American Rose Society, P.O. Box 30,000, Shreveport, LA 71130, U.S.A. Price: $1.00

A.R.S. *Growing Better Roses.* American Rose Society, P.O. Box 30,000, Shreveport, LA 71130, U.S.A.

A.R.S. *Guidelines for Judging Roses.* American Rose Society, P.O. Box 30,000, Shreveport, LA 71130, U.S.A.

A.R.S. *Modern Roses 9.* American Rose Society, P.O. Box 30,000, Shreveport, LA 71130, U.S.A.

A.R.S. *Rose Lover's Guide.* American Rose Society, P.O. Box 30,000, Shreveport, LA 71130, U.S.A.

A.R.S. *What Every Rose Grower Should Know.* American Rose Society, P.O. Box 30,000, Shreveport, LA 71130, U.S.A.

Bassity, Mathew A.R. *The Magic World of Roses.* Heartside Press Inc., Publishers, NY.

Cairns, Dr. Thomas. *Everything You Wanted to Know About Pesticides for Rose Horticulture.* Dr. Thomas Cairns, Chairman, Committee on Product Evaluation, 3053 Laurel Canyon Boulevard, Studio City, CA 91604.

Cavendish, Marshall. *The New Rose Book.* Marshall Cavendish Publications Ltd., 58 Old Compton Street, London, W1V 5PA.

Crockett, James. *Roses.* Time-Life Books, NY.

Drew, John K. *Roses.* A.B. Morse Countryside Publication, Division of the Barrington Press, 200 James Street, Barrington Press, Il.

Editorial Staff of Ortho Books. *All About Roses.* Ortho Books, Chevron Chemical Co., Ortho Division, 575 Market Street, San Francisco, CA 94105.

Editorial Staff of Ortho Books. *The Facts of Light About Indoor Gardening.* Ortho Books, Chevron Chemical Co., Ortho Division, 575 Market Street, San Francisco, CA 94105.

Editorial Staff of the Royal National Rose Society. *Judging Roses, A Handbook for Judges.* The Royal National Rose Society, Bone Hill, Chiswell Green Lane, St. Albans, Herts, England, AL2 3NR.

Editorial Staff of the Royal National Rose Society. *Roses.* The Royal National Rose Society, Bone Hill, Chiswell Green Lane, St. Albans, Herts, England, AL2 3NR.

Editors of Sunset Books and Sunset Magazines. *How To Grow Roses.* Lane Publishing Co., Menlo Park, CA.

Fitch, Charles Marden. *The Complete Book of Miniature Rose*s. Hawthorn Books, Inc., 260 Madison Avenue, New York, NY 10016 (Also, Prentice-Hall of Canada, Ltd., 1870 Birchmount Road, Scarborough, ON).

Gibson, Michael. *Roses in Color.* Orbis Publishing, London.

Harkness, J.L. *World's Favorite Roses and How to Grow Them.* McGraw-Hill Book Co., Maidenhead, England.

Harris, Cyril C. *Beginner's Guide to Rose Growing.* Sphere Books Ltd., 30/32 Gray's Inn Road, London, WC1X 8JL.

Hollis, Leonard. *Roses.* The Hamlyn Publishing Group Ltd., London, New York, Sydney, Toronto.

Kordes, Wilhelm. *Roses.* Studio Vista Ltd., and Blue Star House, Highgate Hill, London, England.

Krussmann, Gerd. *Complete Book of Roses.* Printed in Germany in the German language. It has been translated and now printed (1981) by the Timber Press, P.O. Box 1631, Beaverton, OR 97075, U.S.A. **The best rose book the author has ever read.**

MacCaskey, Michael and Ray, Richard. *Roses, How to Select, Grow and Enjoy.* H.P. Books, P.O. Box 5367, Tucson, AZ 85703.

Malin, Peter and Graff, M.M. *Peter Malin's Rose Book.* Brooklyn Botanic Garden, NY.

McGredy, Sam. *Look to the Rose.* Charles Scribner's Sons, NY.

McGredy, Sam and Jennett, Sean. *A Family of Roses.* The Garden Book Club, 121 Charing Cross Road, London, WC2H 0EB.

Park, Bertram. *Collins Guide to Roses.* Collins, St. James's Place, London, England.

Rockwell, F.F. *Rockwell's Complete Book of Roses.* The American Garden Guild, Inc., and Doubleday & Co., Inc. U.S.A.

Staff of Home Garden's Natural Gardening Magazine. *Book of Roses.* Charles Scribner's Sons, NY.

Taylor, George M. *Pearson's Encyclopedia of Roses.* C. Arthur Pearson Ltd., London, England.

Thomas, Graham Stuart. *The Old Shrub Roses.* J.M. Dent and Sons Ltd., London, England.

Wheatcroft, Harry. *Be Your Own Rose Expert.* Pan Britannica Industries Ltd., Waltham Cross, Herts, England.

## WHAT ROSES TELL YOU (THE IMPLIED MEANING)

Here are some of the most widely accepted **meanings** for the different rose colors, blooms, and arrangements:

- RED ROSES: "I love you." They also stand for respect and courage.

- WHITE ROSES: "You are heavenly;" also purity, reverence, and innocence.

- RED and WHITE TOGETHER: Unity.

- PINK: Grace and/or gentility.

- DEEP PINK: Gratitude and appreciation.

- YELLOW: Joy or gladness. It can also say, "Try to care."

- CORAL or ORANGE: Enthusiasm or desire.

- DEEP BURGUNDY: Beauty.

- RED and YELLOW BLENDS: Happy and jovial feelings.

- PALE COLORS: Convey sociability and friendship.

- ROSE BUDS: Symbolize beauty and/or youth.

- WHITE ROSE BUDS: Girlhood, "Too young to love."

- WILTED WHITE ROSES: Fleeting beauty; you made no impression.

- SINGLE ROSE: Simplicity.

- SINGLE ROSE IN FULL BLOOM: "I love you," or "I still love you."

- BOUQUET OF ROSES IN FULL BLOOM: Gratitude.

- HYBRID TEA ROSES: "I'll remember you always."

- SWEETHEART ROSES: Sweetheart.

- FULLY OPEN ROSE PLACED OVER TWO BUDS: Secrecy.

- TWO ROSES TIED TOGETHER TO FORM A SINGLE STEM: Engagement; a coming marriage.

# GLOSSARY

**acid soil** - soil having a pH of less than 7.0.

**agricultural lime** - soil amendment consisting principally of calcium carbonate, and including magensium carbonate and perhaps other materials. It is used to supply calcium and magnesium as essential elements for growth of plants and to neutralize soil acidity.

**alkali soil** - soil having a high degree of alkalinity (pH of 8.5 or higher), or having a high exchangeable sodium content, or both. A soil that contains enough alkali (sodium) to interfere with the growth of most crop plants.

**annual** - plant which completes its life cycle and dies within one year.

**anther** - the upper part of a stamen, which holds the pollen.

**artificial light** - light provided by means other than the sun (e.g., fluorescent tubes, incandescent lamps).

**balling** - a condition whereby a fully developed bud fails to open.

**basal break** - a cane arising from a bud at the base of an old cane.

**bi-color rose** - a rose with two colors, where the color of the top of the petals is different from the reverse side.

**blended color** - two or more colors are uniformly combined.

**blind end** - a cane that terminates with no terminal bud.

**bud** - that stage of development in which the sepals are down, the petals just beginning to unfurl, and the configuration of the center is not usually evident.

**bud union (graft union)** - the place along the lower stem where the bud was originally budded onto the rootstock (usually visible as a slight swelling on the stem).

**calyx** - the outer parts of a flower called sepals, which are green in a rose.

**chlorosis** - lack of chlorophyll development causing yellowing or whitening of plant tissue.

**clay** - as a particle-size term: a size fraction less than 0.002 mm in equivalent diameter, or some other limit (geologists and engineers). As a rock term: a natural, earthy, fine grained material that develops plasticity with a small amount of water. As a soil term: a textural

class. As a soil separate: a material usually consisting largely of clay minerals, but commonly also of amorphous free oxides and primary minerals.

**clayey** - containing large amounts of clay, or having properties similar to those of clay.

**climber** - a rose that produces long canes which require support to grow upright.

**coarse texture** - texture exhibited by sands, loamy sands, and sandy loams (except very fine sandy loam). A soil containing large quantities of these textural classes.

**cold hardiness** - condition that must be acquired by perennial plants in order to avoid injury when exposed to freezing temperatures.

**compost** - organic residues, or a mixture of organic residues and soil that have been piled, moistened, and allowed to decompose. Mineral fertilizers are sometimes added. If it is produced mainly from plant residue, it is often called "artificial manure" or "synthetic manure".

**conditioning** - a process used by florists to extend the life of a cut bloom.

**confused center** - refers to the petal formation in the center of the bloom; the petal arrangement lacks symmetry.

**crown** - the point where roots and stems join.

**cultivar** - a group of closely related plants propagated and cultivated from a plant with common origin and similar characteristics. Often used in place of the term variety, although varieties are usually naturally occurring selections of the species.

**cultural control** - prevention or control of pests using non-chemical means.

**cuticle** - tough, waxy covering found on the outside surface of leaves.

**decorative variety** - a rose suitable for garden display, but lacking the excellence of bloom needed for exhibition.

**desiccation** - type of plant tissue injury resulting from extreme moisture loss. In continental climates, it is generally associated with low temperatures and wind.

**disbudding** - removal of unwanted flower buds.

**disease resistance** - ability of a plant to prevent the development of a disease on or in it. Resistance varies from complete immunity to slightly less than susceptible.

**dormancy** - plant state where growth stops. Growth usually resumes when growing conditions are more suitable.

**dormancy rest** - profoundly inactive state displayed by a plant during late fall and early winter. The condition is overcome following exposure to a discrete number of hours of critical low temperature. During dormancy rest, no external growth stimulus can cause active growth.

**double bloom** - blooms possessing more than 20 petals.

**evapotranspiration** - the total loss of moisture from the soil, including that by direct evaporation and that by transpiration from the surfaces of plants.

**exhibition rose** - a rose that when one-half to three-quarters open has classic hybrid tea form; a high center with petals symmetrically arranged in an attractive circular outline. The form may occur in many rose types, not only in hybrid teas.

**fault** - a defect or imperfection.

**fertilizer** - any organic or inorganic material of natural or synthetic origin that is added to soil to supply certain elements essential to the growth of plants.

**fertilizer grade** - expression of the percentage content of the fertilizer given in the order of N-P-K.

**fertilizer ratio** - amount of a fertilizer in relation to another or several other fertilizers (i.e., 27-24-7 indicates a ratio of 3:2:1).

**floret** - an individual bloom in a spray.

**flower head** - the collection of florets and buds that form the inflorescence.

**foundation plantings** - plantings at the base of a structure which tie the structure to the landscape.

**friable** - consistence term pertaining to the ease of crumbling of soils.

**full blown** - a mature, open bloom showing stamens.

**fumigant** - a substance used to disinfect or kill vermin.

**genus (plural: genera)** - a major division within a plant family. Example: all apples are of the genus Malus within the extensive Rosa family. The genus is the first part of the binomial, e.g., Malus baccata.

**graft-union** - point of union occurring when a shoot of one plant is grafted to the stem or root of another.

**grooming** - physical improvement of a specimen by the exhibitor.

**hardening-off** - subjecting plants to adverse conditions such as lack of moisture or nutrients in order to hasten the maturation of tissues and the proper acclimating of tissues to cold temperature.

**hardiness** - the characteristics of a plant that enables it to live through various climatic conditions, especially freezing temperatures.

**heading back** - type of pruning cut that is confined to stems of plants where the distal portion of the stem is removed or headed back to a lateral bud.

**heeling in** - a method of holding nursery plants over safely in the soil for a while until it is convenient or possible to plant.

**hips** - rose seed pods. Some are very ornamental. Others are often used for wine, jam, and jelly making.

**host** - plants from which a parasite obtains nourishment.

**humus** - well-decomposed part of organic matter.

**hybrid** - the plant that results when two different varieties or species are crossed.

**hybridization** - the process of creating a new plant by combining the gametes from two separate species.

**impairment** - a fault or deficiency of a specimen. It may be the result of weather, poor culture, poor grooming, or be inherent in the rose, as in the case of white streaked petals.

**inflorescence** - the general arrangement of flowers on an axis. An inflorescence may consist of one spray or a number of sprays.

**irrigation** - artificial application of water to the soil for the benefit of growing crops.

**larva** - immature, wingless, wormlike creature hatched from an egg which goes through minor changes to form a pupa.

**lateral bud** - bud located on the side of a shoot rather than at the terminal end.

**leach** - removal of materials in a solution. Usually done by washing out with water.

**lime-induced chlorosis** - failure of leaves of broadleaved plants to produce chlorophyll when the amount of free-lime in the soil is sufficient to decrease soil acidity to the point where the availability of iron is interfered with.

**macronutrient** - chemical element necessary in large amounts, usually greater than 1 ppm in the plant, for the growth of plants and usually applied artificially in fertilizer or liming materials. 'Macro' refers to the quantity and not to the essentiality of the element to the plants.

**mat foliage** - leaves with a dull finish.

**maturity** - state reached by woody plants that must be achieved before tissues can be cold hardened for winter.

**micronutrient** - chemical element necessary in only small amounts, usually less than 1 ppm in the plant, for the growth of plants and the health of animals. 'Micro' refers to the amount, not the essentiality of the element to the organism.

**miniature rose** - a small rose plant 15 to 30 cm (6 to 12 in.) tall with foliage and flowers in scale to height.

**mulch** - layer of organic or inorganic material laid on the ground to slow moisture evaporation, prevent erosion, and control weeds.

**mulching** - placing one of a number of materials on the soil surface.

**neutral soil** - soil in which the surface layer, to plow depth, is neither acid nor alkaline in reaction.

**nymph** - juvenile insect resembling an adult which becomes an adult without an intervening pupa stage.

**one-bloom-per-stem** - a specimen with no side buds.

**organic matter** - substances derived from living things.

**ovary** - that part of the flower that produces the seed.

**pathogens** - disease-causing organisms.

**peduncle (pedicel)** - the neck, that part of the stem between the flower and the uppermost leaf.

**perennial** - plant which lives for more than two years.

**perlite** - heat-treated silicate rock used as a growing media.

**pesticide** - substance, usually synthetic, that kills or inhibits a selected type of living thing (e.g., insecticides, herbicides, fungicides, nematicides, ovicides, rodenticides, and biocides).

**petiole** - the stem of the leaf.

**point scoring system** - a means of evaluating a specimen.

**pollen** - contains the sperm, which fertilizes the egg within the ovary to produce seeds.

**proboscis** - extremely slender and sharp, pointed portion of the insects' mouth parts.

**pupa** - intermediate form from larva to adult.

**remontant** - recurrent, blooming more than once during the growing season.

**rhizome** - horizontal underground stem.

**root house (root cellar)** - a place for storing or overwintering certain plants and crops underground. Used in temperate regions; the outdoor covered pit provides darkness, and an even cool temperature beneath the frost line.

**rootstock** - stems or roots of a plant to which scions are grafted.

**rosette** - circular cluster of leaves or other plant organs.

**sand** - as a particle term: soil particle between 0.05 and 2.0 mm in diameter. As a soil term: soil textural class.

**seedling** - young plant that usually only contains its cotyledons or first true leaves.

**semi-double bloom** - blooms possessing between 12 and 20 petals.

**side-dressing** - method of applying fertilizer to soil surface under plants or in trenches beside plants.

**silt** - as a particle term: particle between 0.05 and 0.002 mm in diameter. As a soil term: textural class.

**single-flowered** - a bloom with one row of up to 12 petals.

**soil amendment** - material incorporated into the soil to make it more suitable for plant growth.

**soil organic matter** - organic fraction of the soil; includes plant and animal residues at various stages of decomposition, cells and tissue or soil organisms, and substances synthesized by the soil population.

**soil pH** - the degree of acidity or alkalinity of a soil as determined by means of a suitable electrode or indicator at a specified moisture content or soil-water ratio, and expressed in terms of the pH scale.

**soil reaction** - degree of acidity or alkalinity of a soil, usually expressed as a pH value.

**soil salinity** - amount of soluble salts in a soil, expressed in terms of percentage, parts per million, or other convenient ratios.

**soil texture** - proportion of sand, silt, and clay in a soil.

**species** - a group of roses which have one or more distinctive characteristics.

**specimen** - any stem terminating in a bloom or blooms. This term may be applied to Hybrid Teas, Floribundas, Grandifloras, Climbers, Miniatures, and any other type of rose, one-bloom-per-stem or a spray.

**split center** - refers to the petal formation in the center of the bloom. Instead of the high, pointed center, the petals are arranged forming a cleavage resembling two or more centers.

**spore** - seed-like reproductive structure of a fungi.

**spray** - a group of florets on one main or lateral stem. For exhibition purposes, it must show two or more blooms.

**staging** - tables, supports and other items used for horticultural exhibits.

**stamen** - the male organ of the flower is composed of a thin stalk (filament) and a head known as the anther. The anther is the pollen-bearing organ.

**stigma** - the pollen receptive end of the pistil, the female part on which the pollen is retained.

**stock** - the rooted portion of a plant in which a bud is implanted to form a new plant.

**style** - the stem of the pistil that joins the stigma to the ovary.

**sucker** - shoot arising from underground parts of a plant.

**suckering** - characteristics of some plants to produce new growth from adventitious buds.

**systemic pesticide** - herbicide, fungicide, or insecticide that is absorbed and translocated throughout the plant.

**terminal bud** - bud formed at the end of a shoot that normally heralds the end of extension growth for the season.

**tilth** - physical condition of soil as related to its ease of tillage, fitness as a seedbed, and impedance to seedling emergence and root penetration.

**top-soil** - layer of soil moved in cultivation. The A-horizon. Presumably fertile soil material used to topdress roadbanks, gardens, and lawns.

**transpiration** - release of water vapor from living tissues of the plant.

**transplant** - plant that is moved from one location to another. Can also denote the action of transferring a plant from one growing medium to another.

**vermiculite** - a sterile expanded mica medium, light brown in color, commonly used for improving the moisture and air-holding capacity of soil mixes.

**water table** - the level at which the soil is water saturated.

**wettable powder (WP)** - a pesticide in powder form that is suspended in water during application.

# INDEX

## INDEX *(CONTINUED)*

## INDEX (CONTINUED)

## INDEX *(CONTINUED)*